Wales from the Air

Wales from the Air
history in the hills

Paul R. Davis

LOGASTON PRESS

COVER: The spectacular Iron Age hillfort of Pen-y-crug appears out of a sea of fog in the Usk valley near Brecon
FRONTISPIECE: The ruins of Dolbadarn Castle with Llyn Padarn and the peaks of Eryri in the background

First published 2024 by Logaston Press
The Holme, Church Road, Eardisley HR3 6NJ
www.logastonpress.co.uk
An imprint of Fircone Books Ltd.

ISBN 978-1-910839-69-0

Designed and typeset by Richard Wheeler in 11 on 14.5 Garamond.
Cover design by Richard Wheeler.

Printed and bound in Poland www.lfbookservices.co.uk

Logaston Press is committed to a sustainable future for our business, our readers and our planet.
The book in your hands is made from FSC® certified paper.

FSC
www.fsc.org
MIX
Paper from
responsible sources
FSC® C105618

British Library Catalogue in Publishing Data.
A CIP catalogue record for this book is available from the British Library.

Contents

1

Introduction

PEOPLE HAVE BEEN living in Wales for a very long time. A quarter of a million years is the current estimate; but it was not until much closer to our own age that settlers began arriving in greater numbers to farm the land and to build monuments that satisfied their social needs and religious beliefs – monuments that have endured to this day.

Almost every corner of Wales has been touched by these long-departed people, and not just the rich agricultural pastures as might be expected, but seemingly inaccessible islands, windswept coastal cliffs, barren moors, dark caverns – even the bare summits of the highest peaks. All of these places, and more, have revealed the presence of people and their unstoppable urge to leave a mark on the landscape.

The archaeological and architectural heritage of this country encompasses a period of about 6,000 years, from the time the early settlers raised up their mysterious monoliths, through to the fortifications built by warring Celts and Roman conquerors, and on to the towering edifices that tested the skills of the medieval craftsmen to their limits. This legacy of sites and monuments can be enjoyed by

residents and visitors alike, whilst walking, riding or driving through the countryside; but a more unique experience is offered by the airborne camera. A bird's-eye view makes sense of landscape features that might be undetected, or seem insignificant to the passer-by; and can furthermore unravel the tangle of 'lumps and bumps' in a field that signal the activities of the people who have made Wales their home throughout the centuries.

For archaeologists, aerial photography is a valuable tool and a non-invasive way of locating new sites, as well as a means to monitor changes to the historic environment caused by modern agriculture, urban expansion, natural erosion and (regrettably) deliberate vandalism. For the last hundred years the aeroplane has reigned supreme as the way to get the photographer and his camera up in the air, but within the last decade a rival has appeared on the scene, one that offers a far quicker, cheaper and more convenient means to undertake that task – drone photography.

Within these pages will be found a compilation of aerial views taken in recent years, utilising this new technology. This book is not intended as an exploration of the various hi-tech gadgets and computer programmes that form the armoury of the modern photographer, nor is it an in-depth study of the archaeological origins of Wales – it is an overview of the early history of this country told through images; images of the more striking and unusual constructions that can still be seen in the landscape today. The monuments and buildings included here range in date from late-Prehistoric times up to the start of the Early Modern period (roughly from about 4000BC to AD 1500), and include burial mounds, stone circles, hillforts, boundary dykes, deserted farmsteads, churches, monasteries and castle ruins.

The selection of images is a personal one and rather eclectic. A few of the monuments date from outside the chronological bookends noted above, but as they show continuity of use and similar morphology, their inclusion here is justified. Also, one or two have been sneaked in from across the border; however, this too is excusable since the boundary between England and Wales was fluid for a very long time and was only resolved with administrative precision in Tudor times.

Certain historical periods may seem to be poorly represented in these pages, but this is not necessarily due to a lack of relics surviving from that age; it is simply because they do not photograph well from the air. Also, some readers might query why this, or that, well-known landmark has not been included. The intention has not been to provide a series of postcard views of the most famous monuments, but rather to create a visual impression of the way the past has impacted on the countryside – and sometimes an unfamiliar site can create a far more intriguing and striking image than a familiar one.

THE ADVANTAGES OF AERIAL PHOTOGRAPHY

It might be argued that the ancient monuments and historic buildings of Wales were never meant to be seen from the air. For whatever reasons they were built – whether to inspire awe and devotion, to honour and commemorate the dead or to impress and intimidate the living – they were intended to be viewed by anyone approaching on foot. There is no doubt that the alternative vantage of an aerial photograph, while never envisaged by the original builders, can help the modern viewer gain a better appreciation of the monument under scrutiny.

Images captured by the airborne camera take several forms. General views of landscapes, townscapes and upstanding buildings can be taken at almost any time of the day or season of the year, usually with revealing results (Figs 6.23, 6.56 & 6.59 for instance). When the photograph is taken from directly overhead, the ground-plan of the roads and buildings appear almost like a two-dimensional map, but taken at an angle (obliquely) the image shows more features and provides enough of the background to enable the eye to get a sense of perspective and scale.

But what about the much slighter vestiges of mounds, ditches, banks, earthworks and half-buried foundations? – how are these to be photographed effectively? Such subtle archaeological features are often difficult to comprehend from ground level, and only make sense when they are seen from above, highlighted by the interplay of light and shadow.

Take for example, the ground view of Caerau Gaer at Moylgrove near Cardigan (Fig. 1.1a). The ramparts of this large hillfort have been so worn down by centuries of erosion, cattle treading and intensive ploughing, that to the passer-by they appear as insignificant terraces in a field. However,

Figs 1.1a & **1.1b** The earthworks of Caerau Gaer seen from the ground (above) and from the air (right)

the aerial view (Fig. 1.1b), taken from a height of 100m, combined with a low January sun, clearly shows the denuded earthworks to be a series of concentric ramparts encircling the central living area of the fort. Features highlighted by the sun in this way are called **shadowmarks**, and they are best photographed in winter or early spring when there is little undergrowth or leaf cover to obscure the view, and when the sun is usually at a low angle throughout the day. At other times of the year such ideal lighting conditions are restricted to early mornings or late afternoons.

To take a really effective shot of a shadowmark site, the photographer needs to understand the layout of the land around the monument, and how the relative position of the sun will affect the final result. Some monuments (such as those of circular plan) can be photographed on a sunny day from just about any angle with effective results – but other sites may not have such a symmetrical layout

and will only reveal their 'good side' to the camera when the sun is shining from a certain direction. For instance, the earthworks in Figs 3.21, 3.32 & 4.9 would not show up so well if the light was coming from a different part of the sky.

To capture most of the images in this book it was necessary to plan in advance, using Ordnance Survey maps and internet satellite views, to decide the best time of the day to be there. In some cases, the ideal view was only achievable at a specific time of the year. The sun only shines fully on the north side of Chepstow Castle during the Midsummer months, and therefore Fig 6.21 was taken on a June evening, fortuitously coinciding with a high tide on the River Wye. However, things do not always go to plan, and I have spent many an hour on a windswept mountain top impatiently waiting for the sun to break through the clouds, just so that the earthworks will be illuminated at the optimum angle for the photograph to work.

But what can be done about those archaeological sites that have left no surface features at all, having been wiped off the landscape by years of intensive agricultural ploughing? How can they ever be photographed? Under favourable conditions, even these vanished sites can reveal their existence through the effect they have on the ground that covers them. Antiquarians had long observed strange markings that periodically appeared and disappeared in fields and meadows, but the cause of this phenomenon was not fully understood until comparatively recently. It has since been discovered that this is the result of buried archaeological features impacting the crops growing over them.

When artificial features such as pits and ditches become disused and infilled with soil, any crops planted above will benefit from the deeper and moister growing medium; they will ripen slower than adjacent plants and stay greener for longer. Where there is buried stonework the opposite effect occurs – plant growth is stunted, and the crops tend to ripen quicker. The patterns of light and dark patches thus created are termed **cropmarks**. This effect also depends on weather patterns and growing conditions, and may not be visible every season. Furthermore, the natural underlying geology can create similar markings, which can sometimes fool observers into thinking them to be of archaeological origin.

Drought conditions exacerbate the process, so that even grass can produce the same visual effect as deep-rooted cereal crops, leaving pale, parched strips above buried walls and lusher patches where the soil retains some moisture. These are called **parchmarks**. The ghostly outlines of many lost monuments were revealed in this way during the exceptionally hot summer of 2018.

A somewhat similar method of detecting ploughed-out archaeology is through **soilmarks** caused by disturbances of the ground, particularly during heavy ploughing, which can expose differences in the colour of the earth. Typically, soil in buried ditches tends to have a larger content of organic remains and looks darker than the surrounding earth, while the makeup of banks and mounds appears lighter.

The next stage is to interpret the remains captured on the aerial photograph. Cropmarks and parchmarks can be difficult to understand in advance of excavation because they are only *indirect* impressions, and there may be no physical remains left to study on the ground that help with their classification. However, this is not always the case, as the photographs of Brecon Gaer show (Figs 1.2a & 1.2b). The characteristic 'playing card' layout of this Roman fort is clearly marked by excavated walls and a line of mature trees; however, the August heatwave of 2022 created parchmarks that indicate the position of many internal features that have not seen the light of day since they were excavated by archaeologists in the 1920s.

One of the benefits of modern digital photography is the ease with which the colour-balance can be manipulated, so that ephemeral features such as cropmarks and parchmarks can be more readily seen. Opposite is an unaltered colour view of the fort looking northwards (Fig. 1.2a), with the pale lines of buried buildings and roads showing up in the parched ground. The same photo (Fig. 1.2b) has been converted below into a black-and-white image and the contrast increased, so that the details become clearer. The gravelled roads criss-crossing the interior are quite obvious, as are the outlines of many internal buildings, including

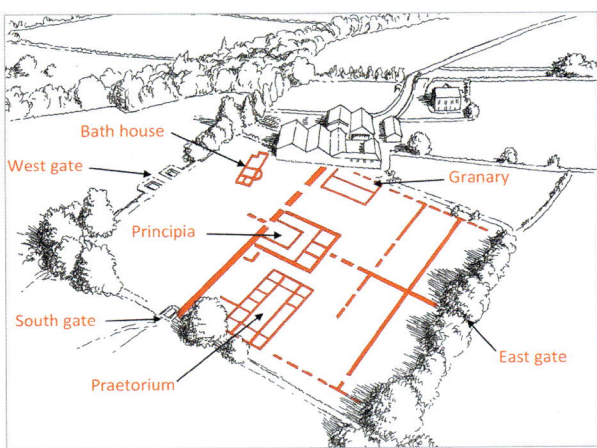

Figs 1.2a & 1.2b Parchmarks revealing the layout of Brecon Gaer Roman fort, near Aberyscir. Fig. 1.2c An interpretive drawing of the site, with the main structures highlighted in red

Labels in Fig. 1.2c: Bath house, West gate, Granary, Principia, South gate, East gate, Praetorium

a small bath-house, the central headquarters block (*principia*), and the adjacent commander's house (*praetorium*). Fig. 1.2c shows a reconstruction drawing of the site.

The photographs on the following pages are mainly of surviving and upstanding structures, or of crisply-defined shadowmarks, so that in many cases it is clear what the building was (a castle or church for instance) and the purpose it would have served. Other sites have such a distinctive appearance that they can be classified with a reasonable degree of confidence (such as a Roman fort). But there are some sites that defy easy interpretation and, without backup information such as datable finds or documentary evidence preserved in historical records, then it can be very difficult to work out what they were used for, let alone to which historical period they might belong. One might hazard a guess as to what they could have been (by comparing them to similar and more reliably dated monuments) but it would still be speculation. However, as a *very* broad rule of thumb, circular or rounded structures tend to be of prehistoric date, while those of angular or rectangular plan are likely to be Roman or medieval.

A BRIEF HISTORY OF AERIAL PHOTOGRAPHY

The use of images recorded from an aerial viewpoint goes back a long time, although it was centuries before it was possible for anyone to leave the ground and return in one piece. Despite this, artists and engravers created remarkably detailed bird's-eye views of major towns and cities in Tudor times, and eighteenth-century antiquarians produced overhead panoramas of the ancient monuments they were busy digging up.

Fig. 1.3
This dramatic 1643 engraving of Hohentwiel Castle in Germany shows the fort from the ground and from the air. Needless to say, the artist was not actually sketching away whilst suspended in the air, but merely has transposed the visible features into an imagined bird's-eye view of the castle

However, these were all *imaginary* views, taking an object visible on the ground and then drawing it as it might look if seen from above. To actually get someone up in the sky was another matter altogether. The ancient Chinese had sent volunteers up into the clouds tied to large kites (usually as a form of punishment), and Leonardo da Vinci drew prototype helicopters and gliders that probably only ever took flight in his head. In the 1780s the invention of the lighter-than-air balloon made it a fashionable novelty for brave people to risk an ascent and get a panorama of the surrounding countryside. This new technology enabled artists and map-makers to draw the landscape below 'from life' for the benefit of their earthbound compatriots. But whatever commercial purposes these early pioneers may have had for their new airships, the economics and practicalities meant that the continuing development of manned flight lay with the military governments of the day. The majority of technological advances of powered flight and flying machines (even the present-day drone technology), have been geared towards the less altruistic requirements of surveillance and warfare.

From the 1840s the skill and imagination of the artist began to be rivalled with the invention of the camera. Nevertheless, decades were to pass before the new technology was sufficiently advanced for decent aerial photographs to be taken. Shutter speeds had to be increased and exposure times shortened to enable a reasonable image to be taken from a swaying basket suspended under a balloon, which might either be tethered to the ground or drift over the countryside at the mercy of the wind. It is considered that the earliest *successful* attempt to photograph the British landscape from a balloon dates from 1863.

Fig. 1.4
A humorous lithograph by Honoré Daumier, of the pioneering aerial photographer Nadar (1820–1910) taking views of the Parisian cityscape

Other ways of taking photographs from the air involved the use of kites, steerable airships and firework rockets that released time-delayed cameras on parachutes. An even more bizarre method was tried out in Germany in 1907 when miniature cameras were strapped onto pigeons! The balloon still remained the most reliable means of taking photos in the air. In Britain, the earliest surviving view of an archaeological site (rather than a general landscape or cityscape) is believed to be a series of photos of Stonehenge taken in the summer of 1906 by Lieutenant P.H. Sharpe from an army balloon tethered over Salisbury Plain.

Technology, however, was constantly on the move. Just three years earlier in America, the brothers Orville and Wilbur Wright had made their first tentative flights in a heavier-than-air machine, heralding the dawn of the modern aeroplane. Britain had to wait until October 1908 for the first plane to leave the ground and make a brief excursion into the air above Farnborough. As before, it was warfare that served as the catalyst for future developments, particularly as the sheer cost of chartering a plane for recreational use was prohibitive for all but the very well-to-do.

The period between the two World Wars saw the rise of aerial photography as a serious tool to complement the archaeologist's trowel. Osbert G.S. Crawford was the pioneer in this field, using images recorded by the Royal Air Force in the 1920s in order to produce his groundbreaking study, *Wessex from the Air* (1928). This book revealed the enormous potential of the airborne camera in archaeological work, and it was Crawford who coined the term 'cropmark' to describe the unusual patterns that periodically appeared in cultivated fields.

In 1948 the Cambridge University Committee for Aerial Photography (CUCAP) was formed, and under the direction of another RAF wartime veteran, J.K. St Joseph, a campaign of aerial surveillance was carried out over much of Britain. The CUCAP collection currently has almost half a million images on file, taken between 1945 and 2009. These images still appear today in archaeological books and journals, and not only serve to show the monuments as they stood at the time, but in many cases reveal a landscape that has been totally transformed with the building of modern roads, motorways and housing.

Aerial photography was another aspect of the investigative work carried out by the four Archaeological Trusts of Wales (Clwyd-Powys, Dyfed, Glamorgan-Gwent, Gwynedd) established by the government in the 1970s. Then in 1983 the National Heritage Act created three departments to preserve and promote the heritage of Britain, and Wales fell under the remit of Cadw: Welsh Historic Monuments (now known simply as Cadw).

Despite the costs involved in hiring a plane, growing interest in aerial reconnaissance for archaeological purposes was given a boost by the large number of discoveries made during the dry summer of 1984. Two years later the Royal Commission on Ancient and Historic Monuments for Wales (RCAHMW) took the step of appointing a full-time aerial archaeologist, and Chris Musson became the first Investigator for Aerial Survey. Since 1997 that position has been taken on by Toby Driver. The Aberystwyth headquarters of the RCAHMW now holds the national archive of aerial photography of Wales, comprising historic views of the Welsh countryside taken by the RAF and by the pioneering company Aerofilms Ltd (founded in 1919). The collection includes the results of the Commission's own ongoing programme of aerial recording, and these images can be viewed on their website (www.coflein.gov.uk).

Another valuable tool that has come into its own in recent years is the 3-D digital laser scanning known as LiDAR (or, as it is more usually spelled, lidar). This is an acronym for Light Detection and Ranging, and although the basic process has been around since the 1960s, its potential for archaeological work has only been fully appreciated within the last 20 years or so. Lidar basically involves bouncing laser beams off the Earth's surface from an aircraft passing overhead, so that accurate, high-resolution models of the ground can be created (Fig 1.5). The results may not be as picturesque as a traditional photograph, but lidar

Fig. 1.5 A lidar image of the centre of Cardiff, showing the rectangular outlines of the Roman fort

has the advantage of being able to 'see' through undergrowth and dense tree cover, and build up a picture of objects that would otherwise remain hidden from the lens of an airborne camera. Also, the computer image can be manipulated so that shadowmark details appear in directions that would never be possible in the real world.

EYE IN THE SKY

Within the last decade, the way that photographers might obtain aerial images has been completely transformed by the appearance of the commercial and recreational drone. No longer is it necessary to resort to the costly option of hiring a plane or a helicopter. Drones – or, to give them their more formal term, Unmanned Aerial Vehicles (UAVs) – are pilotless flying machines usually fitted with a camera, and controlled remotely by an operator on the ground.

Fig. 1.6 A DJI Phantom 'quadcopter' in action

As with other flying machines, drones owe their origins to military inventiveness and have a surprisingly long history (unmanned bomb-filled balloons dropped out of the skies way back in 1849). However, it was not until 2006 that the US Federal Aviation Administration (FAA) authorised their use for commercial and recreational purposes, and in the same year a company named DJI was founded in China, soon to become the largest drone manufacturer in the world. The iconic design of the DJI Phantom 'quadcopter' (a UAV with four propellers) was released in 2013 and has continued to be refined over subsequent years. Sleeker and more compact designs soon followed, some weighing less than 300g and small enough to fit into the palm of your hand. Other companies have joined the fast-moving drone market, offering a wide range of competing makes and models for the enthusiast to choose from.

In such a short space of time, UAVs have become part of modern life, whether used for sport or hobbies, surveying land and buildings, shooting videos for film and TV, crime surveillance or even transporting goods and medical supplies to remote areas. They are easy to use, far more environmentally friendly than an aeroplane, and are evidently here to stay (despite occasional incidents of misuse and flurries of negative publicity). Some organisations and landowners currently restrict the use of drones on their lands, but if they are operated safely, respectfully and within the law, then there should be few issues with their continued use. The problems only arise when the system is abused – but that is relevant to any mechanical device, whether it be a car or a penknife.

The regulations governing the commercial and recreational use of UAVs seem to change with each passing year as the law keeps pace with rapidly advancing technology. Although Britain is no longer part of the European Union, the EU laws have been adopted since January 2021. This is not the place to explore them in detail, but it is expected that anyone who operates a drone should be familiar with the current rules and abide by them (for further information see the Civil Aviation Authority website: www.caa.co.uk).

Despite the convenience and economic benefits of UAVs, they do have limitations when compared to an aeroplane. For a start, there are the legal requirements that define the distances to be kept from buildings and people (for obvious safety reasons). They must not be flown further than 500m from the operator and no higher than 120m above ground level. Such rules can restrict their effective use in built-up areas, but have less impact in the open countryside. However, while it is easy within these restrictions to photograph a fairly small monument, a larger site poses a problem, for it may not be possible to rise high enough

Figs 1.7a & 1.7b Another advantage of digital photography is the ease with which images can be manipulated. These two views show Great Castle Head promontory fort near Dale in Pembrokeshire. Top shows the site as it now appears, disfigured by a natural landslip cutting across the interior; while at the bottom, the damage has been digitally repaired and the earthworks restored to their original level

to capture the whole object in frame, forcing the photographer to rely on a very oblique view. Aeroplanes fly much higher than drones, so that the camera can capture a near-vertical shot that encompasses the whole subject.

More importantly, the airborne photographer has the opportunity to 'window-shop' over a panoramic landscape, and can spot a greater number of sites during flight times, in particular subtle cropmarks in a field. This advantage is denied to the ground-based drone operator, who must physically move to a different location in order to undertake a separate flight. On the plus side, drones can get much closer to a site or a building than a plane ever could. So, for the foreseeable future, a drone is far more likely to complement, rather than usurp, the role of the airborne photographer.

Finally, regarding the photographic section of this book. The following pages have been arranged into the usual divisions into which historians have divided the cultural ages of humankind. Place-name spellings have been derived from the most current edition of the Ordnance Survey maps (so if there are any errors, please blame the cartographers). If a site has a variant name, then I have used the one in common usage. Each featured photograph has been provided with a grid reference so that it can be plotted on an OS map for reference or intended visits; however, please be aware that the inclusion of a site does not automatically mean there is public access to it. Most *are* accessible in some way (they may be managed by Cadw for instance, often situated on designated open access land or else are crossed by public footpaths) but others are privately owned, and should you want a closer look then permission should be obtained from the landowner. Lastly, please remember that most of these sites are Scheduled Monuments, which means they are protected by law and should not be disturbed or damaged in any way. Further information on the individual monuments and other archaeological sites in Wales can be obtained from the aforementioned Coflein website of the RCAHMW.

OPPOSITE: Bronze Age megalith of Maen Llia on a mountain pass through Bannau Brycheiniog (Brecon Beacons)

The Ages of Stone & Bronze
(c.4000–800bc)

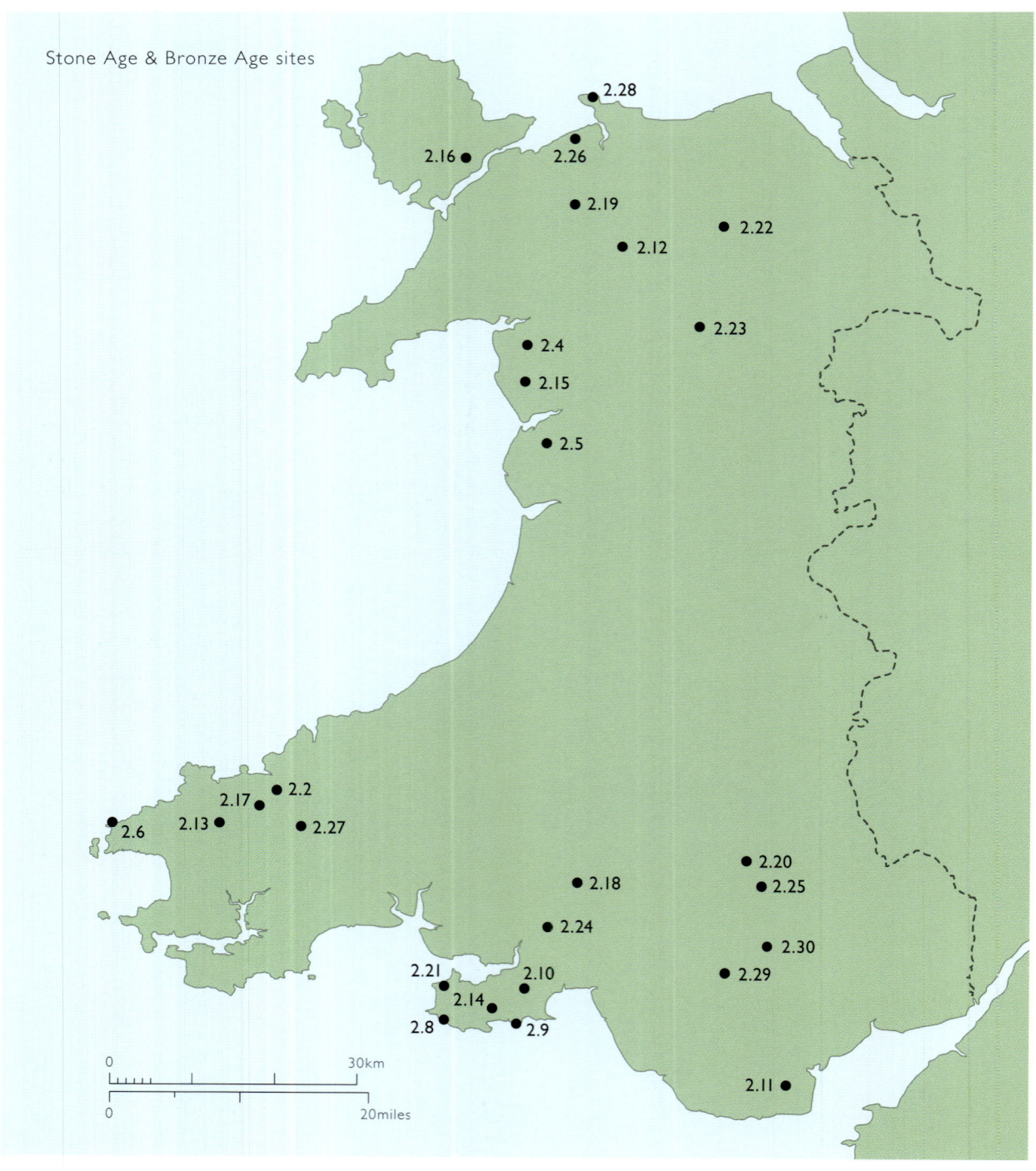

Stone Age & Bronze Age sites

2.28

2.16 ●   2.26

          2.19

               2.22 ●
          2.12 ●

               2.23 ●

     2.4 ●

     2.15 ●

     2.5 ●

                    2.2 ●
          2.17 ●   2.20 ●
2.6 ●   2.13 ●   2.25 ●
          2.27 ●
                         2.30 ●
               2.18 ●   2.29 ●

               2.24 ●

2.21 ●   2.10 ●
     2.14 ●
2.8 ●   2.9 ●
                         2.11 ●

0   30km

0   20miles

For around a quarter of a million years, people have occupied the land we now refer to as Wales. This was the Prehistoric Age, a vast period of time before written records began, but which historians have conveniently subdivided into several distinct phases, based on the type of tools used by early humans.

The people who first came to Wales were not permanent residents, but small groups moving around on a seasonal basis and exploiting the natural resources available – hunting for food in the abundant forests, fishing in the rivers and shallow coastal waters, cutting timber for use as fuel and for building simple shelters. Although they lived in the countryside we now call Wales, these people could hardly be called Welsh, for it would be thousands of years before 'Welshness' as a cultural and social reality would come into existence. Even the land itself had no boundaries that might be compared to a modern map. Virtually no trace has been left of these unknown pioneers apart from the objects found during excavations of their campsites, their tools made from stone, flint or bone – the detritus of their daily existence.

Settlement was undoubtedly periodic, and could only occur when the Ice Age loosened its grip on the Northern Hemisphere; the vast glaciers ebbing and flowing over the course of several millennia. During a period of milder weather around 230000BC, a group of Neanderthal descendants sought refuge in a limestone cave as far north as the Vale of Clwyd; and then, about 33,000 years ago, a group of 'modern' humans sheltered in the limestone crags of the Gower peninsula. When one of their members died, his body was buried in a cave in the cliffs of Paviland (see Fig 2.8), the bones being discovered by an archaeologist thousands of years later. At that time, Gower was not the rugged coastline it is today, but an inland escarpment overlooking a fertile plain – an ideal location for hunting the beasts that provided meat and materials for clothing.

As the climate improved, forests spread over the ice-scoured landscape, and by 8000BC the vast quantity of seawater released from the thawing ice caps had caused a rapid rise in sea levels, isolating Britain from mainland Europe. Henceforward, the nomadic hunter-gatherer groups would be forced to get here by means of primitive boats. No actual surviving buildings or structures are known to have endured above ground from this distant period, and so we must move forward in time to find physical traces left by the early settlers.

Around 6,000 years ago a farming revolution spread to Britain. There is growing evidence that the process of taming the wilderness had started much earlier, and that the hunter-gatherers would stay in one place if conditions were suitable; but it is from the **Neolithic** or New Stone Age (*c.*4000–2300BC), that people undertook more concerted efforts to farm the land. Clearing the dense forests and building homes gave their colonisation a sense of possession and permanency. While their actual dwellings survive only as slight foundations and post-holes uncovered by archaeologists, the houses they erected to revere their dead still survive today, simply because they were built on a monumental scale from materials capable of withstanding the passage of time.

Neolithic burial chambers were constructed using huge stones (megaliths) to form repositories for the bones of their ancestors, and these chambers may also have served to indicate land ownership and territorial boundaries. The burial chamber itself was formed from upright slabs roofed over with a massive capstone weighing many tonnes, with the whole structure then enclosed within a mound of earth (a **barrow**) or of stones (a **cairn**). The covering mound was sometimes of rounded plan, but more commonly was an elongated, wedge-shaped construction. At the entrance end of some mounds there was a forecourt area that seems to have been used for ritual purposes, perhaps for ceremonies connected with the opening or closing of the tomb? From the forecourt a low, stone-lined passageway offered the only way into the burial chamber, so that bones could be deposited inside when necessary (Fig. 2.1). By today, the covering mound has usually been denuded by natural erosion or

Fig. 2.1 Reconstruction of an internment taking place at Pentre Ifan burial chamber

Fig. 2.2 Pentre Ifan today

robbed away by subsequent inhabitants of the land for use elsewhere; but the main megaliths of the chamber – too massive to be easily moved – remain in stark isolation (Fig. 2.2). At two Anglesey sites – Bryncelli Ddu (see Fig. 2.16) and Barclodiad y Gawres – the monuments featured decorated stones in their design, rare examples of Neolithic ritual art. After being excavated, both tombs have had their covering mounds restored (albeit only partially at the former), so that the modern visitor can get an idea of their original appearance.

Neolithic settlers left other traces of their activities in the landscape, showing they could interact with neighbours and invest their resources in undertaking communal enterprises. They built ceremonial enclosures known as **henges**, consisting of a circular bank and ditch earthwork, often containing a setting of upright stones or wooden posts. The term 'henge' is somewhat misleading since it derives from the 'hanging stones' seen at the world-famous site of

Fig. 2.3 A modern recreation of a timber circle, at Worth Matravers (Dorset)

Stonehenge (and nowhere else). It is known that pits and post-holes found at some excavated Neolithic ritual sites held massive upright timbers, and perhaps some were also topped with lintels, rather like the small modern recreation in Dorset seen in Fig. 2.3. Henges are not easy to distinguish from other, later enclosures, unless datable evidence is gleaned from excavation. It has been noted though that henges usually have the ditch on the *inside* of the bank, rather than the outside. Such an arrangement would have severely impacted upon their effectiveness as fortifications, and point instead to a ceremonial use. Other Neolithic earthworks include **Causewayed Camps**, where the line of the bank and ditch is not continuous but interrupted by short gaps, again making it unlikely that these enclosures were built for defensive purposes.

During the course of the third century BC settlers from the Continent brought with them new customs and beliefs and, more importantly, skills in metal-working. Copper was mined and smelted, before the smiths discovered that by adding tin a harder alloy was created, namely bronze. Much of the source material for this process was obtained from the vast underground copper workings at the Great Orme, Llandudno (see Fig. 2.28). This shining new metal was used for grave goods, tools and ceremonial implements, and has provided historians with a name for this period of history – the **Bronze Age** (*c*.2300–800BC). The relatively simple farming community of the Neolithic gradually evolved into a much more complex society in which a class system is likely to have featured. One obvious indication of this is the change from large communal burial chambers to smaller, individual inhumations (usually of cremated remains) under smaller round cairns and barrows.

Figs. 2.4a & **2.4b** A kerbed cairn in the mountains above Harlech, popularly known as the 'Crown of Thorns'

Bronze Age burial mounds vary considerably in size and design. The most plentiful are the simple dome-shaped heaps of earth or stone, usually covering a central slab-lined burial pit (known as a cist). The mound might be just a few metres across, but a few reached massive proportions: Gop Cairn near Prestatyn is the most extreme example, practically an artificial hill, over 70m across and up to 12m high. Other burial mounds were built to more unusual designs for reasons now lost to us,

in the form of rings, saucers and circular platforms (see Figs 2.16, 2.22 & 2.24). Some incorporate upright slabs in their makeup, which seem far too elaborate to have been mere kerbstones intended to keep the body of the mound in place, and must have had a decorative or ritualistic purpose (Fig. 2.4). Burial mounds were commonly built on high ground, often singly, but also in groups, and they were evidently intended to be seen from afar. They may have distantly overlooked the homes of those who had built them, and perhaps served as visual reminders of their ancestral claim to the surrounding land. However, it is important to appreciate that the great number of ancient sites now surviving in upland areas is merely the chance result of their location far from heavily-populated areas, where they would otherwise be at risk of destruction from industrial or agricultural practices. Cairns and barrows are known to have existed in low-lying areas in great numbers, but centuries of ploughing has eradicated many of them, leaving only cropmarks to denote their former presence.

The Bronze Age also witnessed a proliferation of ritual monuments. This points to an increase in population and a surplus of food (thereby allowing labourers to be redirected from essential agricultural work), but it also indicates that there was a hierarchy with the power and authority to organise such activities. Many of the monuments were doubtless built from timber, which would leave no trace once the wood had rotted away (except as post-holes revealed in archaeological excavations). Only those constructed from natural stone had a better chance of enduring to the present. There are over 1,500 standing stones surviving today in Wales, ranging from a few centimetres in height to massive monoliths over 4m tall (Fig. 2.5).

Fig. 2.5 The standing stone of Ffordd ddu near Arthog in Gwynedd

Fig. 2.6 Hut circles at St David's Head, Pembrokeshire

Fig. 2.7 A modern recreation of Prehistoric roundhouses at St Fagans National Museum of History

Why the stones were erected in the first place is a subject that archaeologists and interested amateurs have puzzled over for a very long time, and the possibility that they were territorial indicators, burial markers or totemic idols, are among the likelier theories. Standing stones are found singly, in pairs, in rows and, occasionally, in company with that most iconic monument of the Bronze Age – the stone circle. It must be admitted that none of the Welsh circles are as spectacular as those in other parts of Britain (Stonehenge and Avebury being the most famous and monumental examples). Few of the stones stand more than 1m high, yet their modest size is offset by the spectacular natural locations in which they were set, and it would appear that the original builders deliberately incorporated aspects of the surrounding landscape into the design and function of their monuments (see the Druids Circle, Penmaenmawr, Fig. 2.26).

From this period too, the earliest settlement sites have survived above ground. Although Neolithic builders seemed to prefer houses of rectangular plan

(as we do today), for thousands of years, Prehistoric dwellings were almost invariably built to a circular plan containing one main living space. The walls would have been constructed either from perishable materials (timber, turf, clay) or from more durable drystone, and the peaked roofs were made of turf or thatch. Most of these early houses have long since decayed away, leaving only the slightest of indentations in the ground; but again, those built from stone tend to be marginally better preserved, being marked by rings of tumbled scree and upright slabs (Fig. 2.6). Modern recreations of ancient roundhouses can be seen at the National History Museum at St Fagans (Fig. 2.7), and Castell Henllys near Cardigan.

Roundhouses were grouped together with paddocks for livestock and larger field enclosures for crop-growing, and were built throughout the Welsh countryside. However, it is in the uplands that they survive in the greatest numbers, and OS maps show hundreds of 'hut circles' and 'settlements' in these areas. As mentioned above, this apparent abundance is likely due to the relatively undisturbed nature of the uplands; however, there is another factor to account for this proliferation, one that we are uncomfortably familiar with today – climate change.

Since the last Ice Age northern Europe has experienced a series of climatic fluctuations that lasted for centuries, and for much of the Neolithic and Bronze Ages the weather was generally milder than it is at present, enabling marginal uplands to be intensively farmed and settled. But from about 1100BC there was a marked deterioration in the climate, which reached its lowest ebb around 600BC, before slowly improving again. This environmental downturn is blamed for certain changes to society and settlement patterns in Britain. Farmsteads were built in more compact and elaborate groupings with a greater emphasis on defence than ever before. As the climate became cooler and wetter, the once populous uplands were less viable for farming. Settlements were abandoned as the population migrated to better land, putting pressure on available resources and competing with established communities. Tensions rose, doubtless causing episodes of

cattle raiding, outbreaks of hostility and sporadic inter-tribal feuding; and this ultimately led to the appearance of the first truly substantial monuments in the landscape.

Fig. 2.8 Paviland Caves, Gower
(SS 437 859). The Gower peninsula is particularly rich in caves occupied during the Palaeolithic (Old Stone Age). The most famous site is on the south coast at Paviland. The larger right-hand opening was the location of one of the earliest scientific excavations of an ancient burial site. The body was accompanied by grave goods (including a mammoth skull) and had been dusted with red ochre. This gave rise to the name 'the Red Lady of Paviland'. Later, it was accepted that the skeleton was actually of a young man, and was far older than realised at the time. The current estimate puts the burial at around 29000BC, making Paviland one of the earliest sites of human occupation in Britain.

Fig. 2.9 Bacon Hole, Gower (SS 560 868). Another cave in the rugged Gower cliffs is Bacon Hole (visible as an arched opening halfway up). This has produced finds showing intermittent occupation in Prehistoric and historic times, but an even more remarkable discovery was made in 1912 – a series of red markings on the wall within the dark recesses of the cavern. This was considered to be the first known example of Prehistoric cave art in Britain, and a metal grille was set up to protect the rare find. Unfortunately, the markings later disappeared, and it is thought they were natural mineral stains. Gower's reputation has, however, been enhanced by the recent discovery of stone carvings at another cave, which is now believed to be the oldest example of rock art in Europe.

Fig. 2.10 Parc Cwm chambered tomb, Gower (SS 538 898). This small Neolithic burial chamber was discovered and excavated in 1869, when the remains of up to 24 individuals were found. It was restored in 1960 to near its original appearance, although the capstones that would originally have roofed the chambers are missing. It is now in the care of Cadw. This high view, looking north-west, shows a number of distinctive features shared by other sites in south-east Wales and Gloucestershire, giving rise to the term 'Severn-Cotswold' tombs, and suggesting a common cultural link. The funnel-shaped forecourt led into an entrance passage with four small side chambers, all covered by a wedge-shaped cairn.

Fig. 2.11 Tinkinswood burial chamber, St Nicholas (ST 093 733). Here in the Vale of Glamorgan near Cardiff is another restored example of the Severn-Cotswold type of Neolithic tomb, although there is just a single chamber under the huge capstone, estimated to weigh 40 tonnes. The site was excavated in 1912 and restored, and is now in the care of Cadw. Although the tomb had been disturbed in the past, archaeologists discovered skeletal remains from at least 50 individuals. The present covering of grass disguises the original covering cairn of stones. A short distance away at St Lythans, the stone chamber of another accessible tomb can be seen in a field beside the road.

Fig. 2.12 Capel Garmon burial chamber, Llanrwst (SH 818 543). This is another example of a Severn-Cotswold tomb, but located far outside the normal zone for such monuments. Was it a relic of a tribe that had made the long journey north to settle within sight of the dramatic peaks of Eryi? The mound has been marked by upright stones following excavation and restoration in the 1920s, but the funnel-shaped forecourt (foreground) is a deliberate dead-end, presumably to confuse grave robbers. The true entrance was through the side of the mound (on the left) which led into the central square chamber. There were two additional burial chambers on either side; one still retains its capstone.

Fig. 2.13 Carn Turne burial chamber, Treffgarne (SN 979 273). Unlike the excavated and conserved tombs seen above, this is how most Neolithic burial chambers survive today, stripped of any covering mound with only the main megaliths upstanding. The enormous capstone of this Pembrokeshire tomb is reputed to weigh 40 tonnes, and has collapsed onto its fallen supporters. Clearly evident from the photo is a V-shaped arrangement of upright slabs that marks the chamber forecourt. Carn Turne is in many ways comparable to the better-known Pentre Ifan (Fig. 2.2), and was evidently the focus of significant Neolithic activity here, as there are two smaller tombs less than one mile away.

Fig. 2.14 Arthur's Stone, Gower (SS 492 906). The capstone of this famous burial chamber is a natural boulder (a glacial erratic estimated to weigh at least 30 tonnes) which was deposited here by a passing glacier during the Ice Age. The Neolithic tomb-builders dug under the stone, propping it up with smaller slabs to create a burial chamber, and then surrounded the whole with a circular mound of rubble. Despite centuries of despoliation, the encircling cairn can still be seen in this view, looking north across the Loughor estuary. According to legend the capstone is supposed to have been a pebble that King Arthur found in his shoe and tossed away.

Fig. 2.15 Carneddau Hengwm, Barmouth (SH 613 205). In contrast to the circular cairn at Arthur's Stone, these paired tombs have a more typical elongated plan, the largest and best preserved being just over 100ft in length, with some features that suggest an affinity with the Severn-Cotswold group. Both cairns have suffered from disturbance and stone-robbing over the years, and there is some uncertainty over the number of burial chambers that once lay within the mounds. The megaliths of one ruined chamber can just be seen in front of the wall cutting across the larger cairn.

Fig. 2.16a & 2.16b Bryncelli Ddu burial chamber, Llanfair Pwllgwyngyll (SH 506 701). One of the most remarkable Neolithic monuments on Anglesey, the site was thoroughly excavated in 1928–9 and afterwards restored (although the covering mound was only replaced over the chamber – it would originally have covered the whole area within the ditch). The long entrance passage is exactly aligned with the Midsummer sunrise, allowing a shaft of light to penetrate into the central burial chamber. It is now believed that Bryncelli Ddu originated around 3000BC as a henge, comprising a bank and ditch enclosure with a ring of upright stones, apparently with a rare, decorated slab at its centre. The original has been taken to the National Museum of Wales (Cardiff), but a copy has been set up on the site (left). Around 1,000 years later the henge was deliberately dismantled when the burial chamber was built over it.

Fig. 2.17 Banc Du enclosure, Maenclochog (SN 061 306). The first recognised Neolithic enclosure in Wales, discovered by RCAHMW aerial reconnaissance in 1990, and confirmed by a small excavation in 2005. It lies in the foothills of the Preseli Mountains of Pembrokeshire and appears to be a two-phase structure, the earlier being an oval bank and ditch enclosure on the summit of the hill (white arrows) with a larger outer enclosure (blue arrows). Radiocarbon dates from material in the silted-up ditch indicated that the site was in existence around 3650BC, and that the earthworks were more substantial than they now appear, with a stone-faced bank and timber posts. The photo was taken on a late April evening looking south-west, with Rosebush reservoir in the background.

Fig. 2.18 Tair Carn Uchaf, Brynamman (SN 694 173). In this view, two of the three Bronze Age burial mounds can be seen, that make up the 'three higher cairns' of the place-name. Another group lies further along the ridge. Despite the remoteness of the setting, the cairns have long been robbed, their interiors scooped out by antiquarians or ramblers pointlessly searching for 'treasure'.

Fig. 2.19 Carnedd Dafydd, Bethesda (SH 663 530). Whoever was buried here around 4,000 years ago must have been very important to have been laid to rest on one of the highest peaks in Wales, at over 3,400ft above sea level. Hikers take a rest in a modern shelter that was probably built from stones pillaged from the adjacent cairn. (Incidentally, this photo was not taken with a drone, but a very long selfie stick.)

Fig. 2.20 Pen-y-Fan cairn, Bannau Brycheiniog (Brecon Beacons) (SO 012 215). At the opposite end of the country to Carnedd Dafydd is another notable peak crowned with a Bronze Age burial mound. At over 880m above sea level, Pen-y-Fan is the highest mountain in South Wales, though it can be reached by a relatively easy path from the Storey Arms car park. That convenience has, regrettably, led to the summit being stripped bare by excessive numbers of walkers. In 1991–2 the cairns on Pen-y-Fan and neighbouring Corn Du were excavated before any sensitive archaeological evidence was lost for good. They were found to have central burial cists and concentric rings of kerbstones, and dated from around 2500–2000BC. The cairns were afterwards rebuilt to ensure their future longevity.

Fig. 2.21 Llanmadoc Hill, Gower (SS 441 926). Another superbly situated burial mound, one of many on this hill at the western end of Gower, with panoramic views over the Loughor estuary. The cairn was originally far larger than the current spread of rubble suggests, and the bizarre 'face' is just the result of walkers rearranging the stones to form shelters.

Fig. 2.22 Llyn Brenig platform cairn (SH 989 565). Many of the Prehistoric sites here were studied and excavated when the reservoir was being built in the 1970s, and this cairn, situated on the east side of the reservoir, was dated to around 1950–1650BC. It contained an adult and child burial, and was originally built as a ring cairn, but the open centre was later infilled to form a disk-like platform of stones. The restored cairn now forms part of the Brenig Archaeological Trail.

Fig. 2.23a Moel Ty-uchaf cairn circle, Llandrillo (SJ 056 372). Superbly located on the edge of the Berwyn Mountains above the Dee valley, this impressive site is often considered to be a stone circle, but is in fact the remains of kerbed cairn, and was probably constructed around 3000–1000BC. The prominent ring of stones, 12m in diameter, may have served to retain a covering mound that has been robbed away, and the central hollow probably marks the site of a despoiled stone coffin, or cist, in which either a body or cremated remains would have been placed. The antiquarian label 'cairn circle' is often used on maps to indicate the remains of such mounds that have highly prominent kerbstones.

Fig. 2.23b Moel Ty-uchaf cairn circle, Llandrillo (SJ 056 372) Another view of the well-preserved cairn circle at Moel Ty-uchaf. There is a similar stone circle (although not so impressively sited), in the valley below, on private land at Tyfos House.

Fig. 2.24 Graig Fawr ring, Pontardulais (SN 628 067). Among the numerous monuments scattered over the Graig Fawr ridge is this curious double ringwork, possibly a ritual enclosure or a despoiled ring cairn. The smaller and more obvious circle at the top right appears to be a later addition, perhaps a hut or sheepfold. The view is seen looking west, and as the earthwork is only a few centimetres high in places, it had to be photographed when the sun was very low in the sky.

Fig. 2.25 Cwm Cadlan ring cairn, Penderyn (SN 984 109). This fine ring cairn lies within the Bannau Brycheiniog National Park (Brecon Beacons), and is one of the best examples in Wales of this type of monument. The stony ring defined a ceremonial or sacred space around a central burial cist, which lies to the right of the figure. There are several other cairns in the locality, as well as the remains of dwelling huts and field walls, indicating that this seemingly bleak upland tract was once intensively settlec when the climate allowed.

Fig. 2.26 Druids Circle, Penmaenmawr (SH 723 746). This is undoubtedly the finest stone circle surviving in Wales today, the upland location only adding to the splendour of the setting. There are many cairns and circles on this ridge, but none are as complete nor as impressive as the so-called Druids Circle. In popular culture, stone circles have become inextricably linked with this mysterious and powerful priesthood of late-Iron Age times, but in reality there was no connection; this monument was built as much as 2,000 years before the Druids rose to prominence. The circle is 35m in diameter and the stones are set into a low circular bank, with an entrance gap in the south-west side (foreground). Excavation in 1958 revealed there was a central cist as well as other cremation internments here, so the circle was used for burials as well as ceremonies. This view is looking north-east towards the Great Orme headland in the distance, an important source of the raw copper for making bronze.

Fig. 2.27 Gors Fawr stone circle, Mynachlog-ddu (SN 134 293). At the other end of Wales, in the foothills of the Preseli Mountains, is another fine Bronze Age circle, comprising a ring of 16 stones, 22m across. The stones are not as conspicuous as those of the Druids Circle (the tallest is only 1.4m high), but again, the landscape seems to have been purposely incorporated into the setting. This view looks north-east towards the rugged outcrop of Carn Meini on the horizon. From the centre of the circle, the alignment is framed by a pair of standing stones (just visible in the middle of the photo, in front of the dark line of trees). Several of the stones are of spotted dolerite (also known as 'bluestone') which probably came from the outcrop. Bluestones from the Preseli uplands certainly feature at the famous monument of Stonehenge, though how they got to Salisbury Plain is a hugely controversial issue – deposited by Ice Age glaciers, or dragged by Neolithic navvies? Perhaps even a bit of both?

Fig. 2.28 Bronze Age mines, Llandudno (SH 769 832). Four thousand years ago, copper-mining began on the limestone headland of the Great Orme. Countless labourers tunnelled into the rock in search of the valuable ore which, when mixed with tin, produced bronze. It is estimated that as much as 200 tonnes of smelted copper was produced here before the works ceased around 600 BC, making this the largest Prehistoric copper mine in western Europe. Mining restarted in the eighteenth and nineteenth centuries, and when the underground workings were rediscovered in the 1980s it was first thought they were Victorian in date, but the existence of stone and bone tools indicated far earlier origins. The extensive network of tunnels and caverns is now a popular tourist attraction. This view looks eastwards over the opencast pit towards the resort of Llandudno, which grew up on the isthmus connecting the Orme to the mainland. At the bottom-left can be seen a carriage making its way to Halfway Station on the tramway that has been carrying visitors up the Great Orme since 1902.

Fig. 2.29 Hen Dre'r Mynydd, Rhondda (SN 923 019). These two views show the type of upland farmsteads that appeared in the later Bronze Age, and persisted through the Iron Age and Roman period, consisting of several stone-built round huts within, or adjoining, a network of walled enclosures and paddocks. They are very difficult to date without good evidence recovered from excavation. Both of these sites are relatively well-preserved, and could have been reused and refurbished by farmers and shepherds over a long period of time. Hen Dre'r Mynydd ('old town of the mountain') is one of the best-preserved hut groups in Glamorgan, and is certainly the most accessible, lying next to the picnic area on the A4061 road between Rhigos and Treherbert.

Fig. 2.30 Cwm Criban hut group, Pontsticill (SO 069 134). A large group of huts and enclosures spread over a wide area of remote moorland north of Merthyr Tydfil. As with Hen Dre'r Mynydd, the age of this monument is uncertain, and the better-defined pens towards the bottom-right suggest it has been reused in medieval or later periods. Nevertheless, the site is typical of the open settlements that exploited the uplands while the good climate lasted. With the advent of wetter weather at the end of the Bronze Age, hill farmers would have struggled to survive in such marginal areas. Many settlements would have been abandoned, although it is possible that some remained in use during the summer months when cattle were taken to the high pastures for grazing.

OPPOSITE: The stone ramparts of Foel Faner hillfort overlook Dolgellau and the Mawddach Estuary in southern Gwynedd

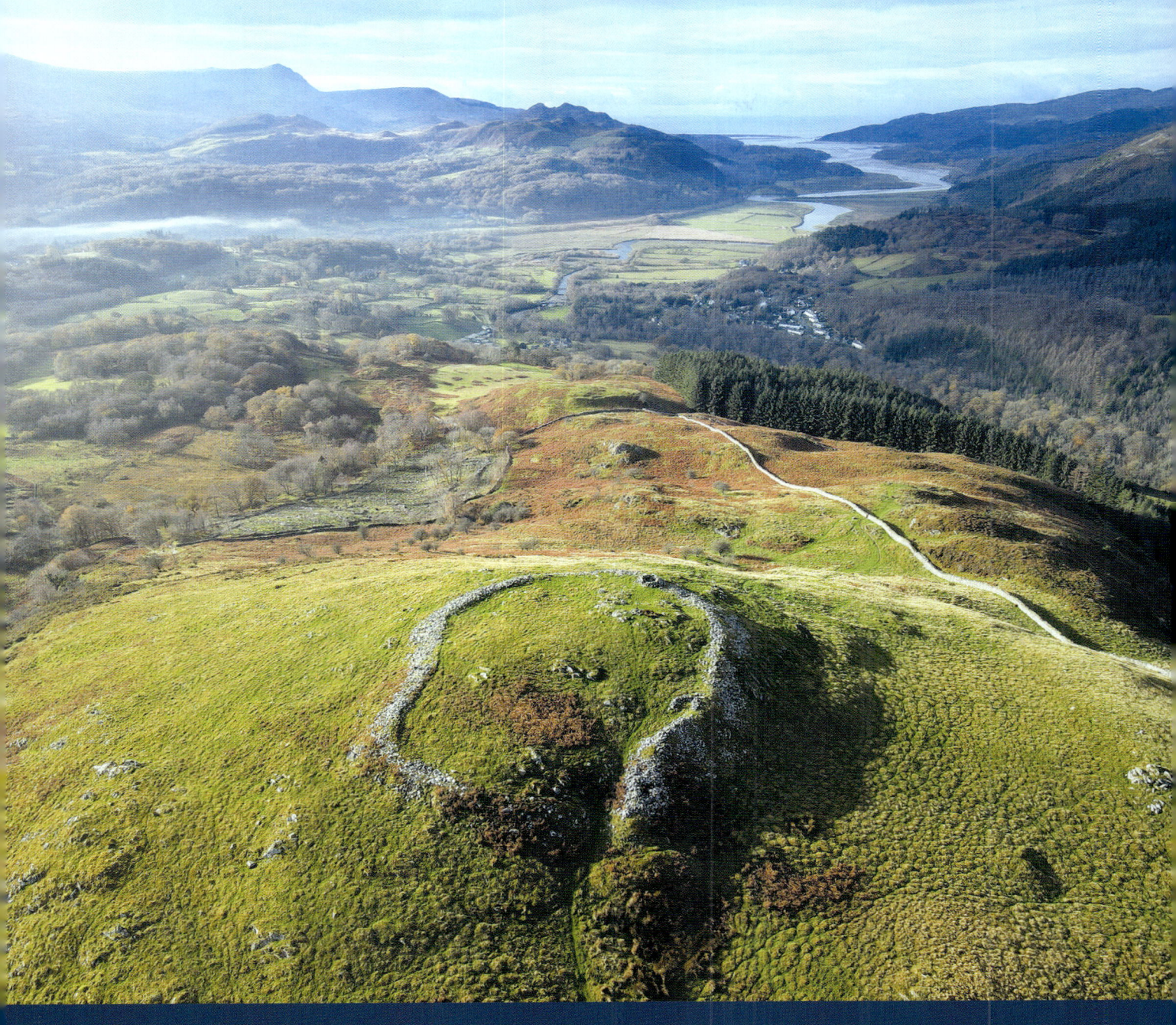

The Age of Iron
(*c.*800BC–AD 43)

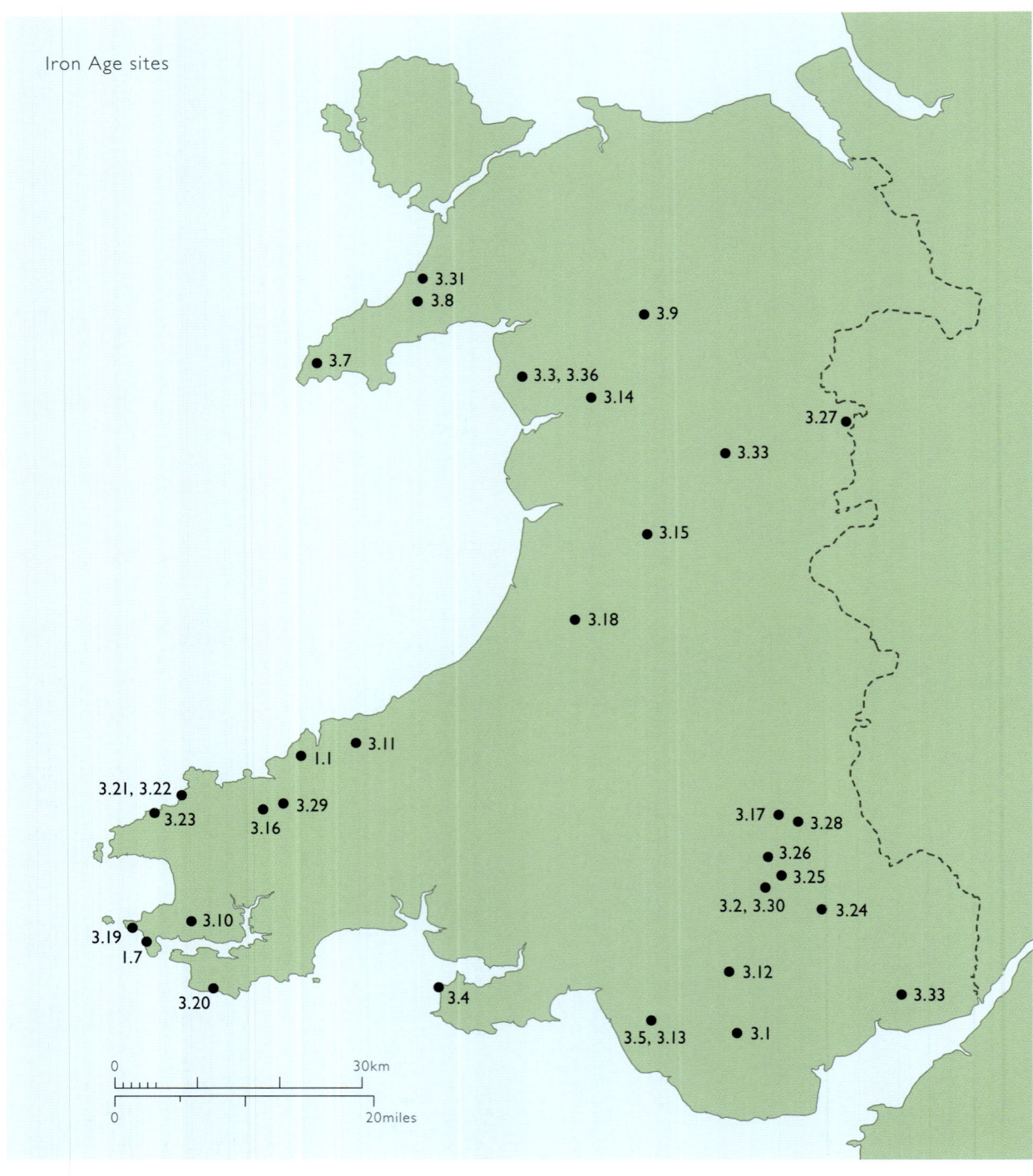

Iron Age sites

3.31
3.8
3.9
3.7
3.3, 3.36
3.14
3.27
3.33
3.15
3.18
3.11
1.1
3.21, 3.22
3.23
3.29
3.16
3.17
3.28
3.26
3.25
3.2, 3.30
3.24
3.10
3.19
1.7
3.12
3.20
3.4
3.33
3.5, 3.13
3.1

0   30km
0   20miles

THE CHANGES THAT afflicted society towards the end of the Bronze Age only intensified as new waves of settlers arrived from central Europe. Known to history as the Celts, these migratory groups shared a similar religion, language and culture. Their skilled craftsmen were renowned for producing implements and intricately decorated objects from gold, bronze and from a more durable metal – iron – after which this period has been named. The Celts also had a reputation for aggression. It was once believed that they swept through the land and brutally displaced the existing communities, but it is now considered far more likely that they arrived in smaller groups over a much longer period of time, gradually merging with the indigenous population until they became the dominant culture in Britain. Compared to the earlier historical eras, the Iron Age spanned a relatively short period of time, perhaps no more than a few centuries, from about 800BC up to the arrival of the Romans in the first century AD. In fact, some historians prefer a much later start date, sometime around 600BC, when the new metal made its first appearance in Wales, and elements of Celtic society certainly lasted long after the Romans came, saw and conquered.

The Iron Age was a time characterised by the construction of earthworks on a scale hitherto unseen in Prehistoric Britain, creating an impact on the landscape that can still be appreciated today. The burial mounds and ritual circles, that had characterised Neolithic and Bronze Age communities, were now overshadowed by the appearance of settlements protected by ramparts of earth and stone. Research has suggested that the use of **hillforts** and defended settlements took place much earlier than the arrivals of the Celts, in response to the unsettled social conditions of the later Bronze Age. It is estimated that over 600 Welsh hills are crowned with the remains of defended enclosures and hillforts, a visual testament to the huge amount of time and effort that went into their construction.

Hillforts generally comprise a living space on the summit of a hill or a ridge, encircled by a series of banks and ditches. A site with a single circuit is termed **univallate** (Fig. 3.1), while larger and more elaborate forts might have two (**bivallate**) or even three or more concentric lines of defence (**multivallate**) (Fig. 3.2). At its simplest form, the rampart might be a dump of earth dug out of a ditch and topped with a hedge or wooden stockade;

TOP: **Fig. 3.1** A univallate hillfort on Mynydd y Gaer, Coychurch
BOTTOM: **Fig. 3.2** The massive multivallate defences of Pen-y-crug near Brecon

Access to the interior of the fort was often a simple gap through the rampart and closed by a wooden gate; but again, the larger the site, the more elaborate the entrance features might be. Many had four-post wooden structures that served as a gateway and carried a parapet and walkway above. The approach could be further strengthened by having the ends of the ramparts overlapping or turned sharply inwards, thereby forcing attackers into a bottleneck and exposing their flanks to the spears and slingstones of the defenders (Figs 3.27 & 3.28). Some sites have what appear to be small guard-rooms built into the entrance passageways, and there are even a few examples of a particularly tricky way of keeping an enemy at bay – *chevaux de frise* ('Frisian horses'): basically a series of upright stones or timber stakes intended to impede a horseback attack or trip up an unwary foot soldier. Although common in parts of Europe and Ireland, only a handful of sites in Wales have retained this elaborate pin-cushion construction, and the best surviving example is at Carn Alw on the moors of the Preseli uplands (Fig. 3.16).

The open space within the hillfort defences would be filled with roundhouses, workshops, animal pens, granaries and food storage pits, all designed to support a population level that, in some cases, must have run into the hundreds. The well-preserved foundations of about 150 huts can be seen within the walls of Tre'r Ceiri (Fig. 3.31), while the larger hillfort of Garn Boduan nearby contains an estimated 170 dwellings. The crowning glory of the Preseli Hills in Pembrokeshire is Foeldrygarn (Fig. 3.29), where the pockmarks of over 220 vanished roundhouses can be seen, squeezed in between the stone ramparts and the three massive Bronze Age cairns on the summit. Whether these

but it could also be a much more substantial construction incorporating timber baulks or drystone revetments for greater stability, with a palisade and wall-walk around the perimeter. In the mountainous parts of Wales, where there was an abundance of good building material, the defences were usually constructed entirely from durable stone, and remain impressive feats of construction, despite 2,000 years of dilapidation.

Fig. 3.3 A reconstruction of a stone-walled hillfort in upland Gwynedd. This is based on Craig-y-dinas (Dyffryn Ardudwy) which has additional outer defences and a walled road approaching the entrance

surprisingly massive defences that appear quite disproportionate to the living space enclosed. Caerau at Abereiddy, is one such example (Fig. 3.23). The complex arrangement of banks and ditches encloses a relatively small and sloping circle of land, offering barely enough room for two or three roundhouses, if indeed that many. While it is possible that the passage of 2,000 years has led to significant coastal erosion, the evidence for this is not convincing at Caerau. However, at other Pembrokeshire sites it is clear that the sea has had a catastrophic effect on the archaeological remains (and, indeed, continues to do so). Porth y Rhaw near Solva and Greenala Point near Stackpole are two major promontory forts that have been eroded to such an extent that, within the ramparts, there is little left except a sheer drop to the sea. At Flimston Bay near Castlemartin, the pounding waves

dwellings were all occupied at any one time, or represent many generations of settlement and abandonment, is a debatable point.

Promontory forts combine the ingenuity of the Iron Age builders with the natural spectacle of the Welsh coastline. The most obvious reason for building a settlement on a headland is to save on the back-breaking labour of digging earthworks, since defences would only need to be built on the side not protected by the natural cliffs. Pembrokeshire has the largest group of promontory forts in Wales, thanks to the county's extensive 186-mile-long coastline of undulating bays and rocky inlets, many of which provided an abundance of suitable locations to occupy.

In an ideal setting, a large headland could be protected with just a few earthworks drawn across the isthmus (Figs 3.4 & 3.21). Some sites have

Fig. 3.4 Burry Holms (Gower) has just a single bank and ditch to impede access to the headland settlement

have not only attacked from the sides, but from *underneath* as well, creating a spectacular chasm in the centre of the fort (Fig. 3.20).

Promontory forts are not only confined to the coast but occur inland as well, wherever a suitable headland or ridge could be found. Again, it was a case of heaping the defences on the side an enemy would be expected to approach. Gaer Fawr (Fig. 3.25) is a particularly extreme example of an inland promontory fort, where multiple ramparts are massed only on the flank vulnerable to attack. The rest of the narrow enclosure had no protection whatsoever apart from the steep natural slopes. It might be assumed that *something* existed along the edge (perhaps a lightweight fence or a hedge), just to give some security and prevent the livestock from slipping over.

In contrast to such massive and obviously fortified sites, there exists a large number of smaller and more lightly-defended settlements, which are not always so well-preserved and, in many cases,

Fig. 3.5 Y Bwlwarcau is one of several settlements with widely-spaced defences on Margam Mountain

survive only as faint earthworks or cropmarks. These enclosures seem too weak to have ever formed a serious obstacle to attack, and their modest stockades must have been built merely to provide peace of mind to the farming family that lived within. They may be more appropriately called farmsteads rather than forts. Some of them have large and widely-spaced outer enclosures that may have been intended for agricultural purposes or to keep their valuable livestock safe from wild beasts and opportunistic raiders. A particularly interesting group of such farmsteads survive on Mynydd Margam in Glamorgan (Figs 3.5 & 3.13). All five share similar features and lie together within a radius of 1.5km. It is tempting to see them as being broadly contemporary – but how did they relate to each other (if at all)? Were they rival settlements, fiercely protective of their own piece of mountainside, or were they affiliated communities living and working together in comparative harmony?

Hillforts and promontory forts offer more questions than easy answers: were they 'palaces' for a warrior elite? Were they temporary refuges for a local community during unsettled times? Were they used all year round, or only occupied seasonally by a populace that lived and farmed elsewhere? Life would have been very hard indeed in an upland hillfort during a typical Welsh winter. What can be deduced from archaeological excavations and the visual evidence of fieldwork, is that many hillforts were not static constructions, but underwent phases of refurbishment, rebuilding and expansion, increasing in scale and complexity as the Iron Age entered its turbulent twilight.

To look at just one example in detail: Castell Odo (Fig 3.7, overleaf) is a modest bivallate enclosure set on a low hill near the tip of the Llŷn

Peninsula (that long arm of land pointing into the Irish Sea). Excavations here in 1958–9 revealed that the site had a complex development barely hinted at by aerial photographs. Sometime between 600 and 300BC the hilltop supported an open settlement of timber roundhouses, which was later enclosed by a wooden stockade (although this was burnt down before it was completed). The site was apparently abandoned for a period, and then reoccupied, this time given a rather feeble encircling bank (the outermost line in the photo). This earthwork was later refurbished, and a much more substantial rampart was built inside it, greatly increasing the defensive strength of the site, although reducing the available living space. Finally, the defences were levelled, and stone roundhouses added, so that Castell Odo ended its days as it had started, as an undefended 'open' settlement (it has been suggested that this latter phase was a direct result of the Roman Conquest of North Wales in the late-70s AD). Another bivallate enclosure at nearby Meillionydd was partially excavated in 2010–15 and similarly revealed evidence for a long period of occupation, stretching from the Late Bronze Age into the Early Iron Age. More recent excavations at Penycloddiau on the Clwydian Hills, have indicated that this enormous 64-acre multivallate fort (one of the largest in Wales) was preceded by a much less monumental wooden stockade.

Some experts consider the term 'hillfort' to be something of a misnomer, a catch-all label that includes sites that were clearly not on a hill nor were strongly fortified. They argue that the forts may not have been intended for practical warfare at all, and point out that few have an adequate water supply that would have made it possible for the inhabitants to outlast a prolonged siege. The suggestion is that

Fig. 3.6 A close-up of the massive boulder walls of Craig-y-dinas hillfort (Dyffryn Ardudwy) that have stood for over 2,000 years

the massive earthworks and elaborate gateways were really intended to be visual deterrents to potential attackers, and to serve as status symbols that boldly displayed the power and prestige of the ruling tribe and its capability in organising such labour-intensive works. Look at the stone-walled citadel of Tre'r Ceiri (Fig. 3.31) and the multiple earthworks of Pen-y-crug (Fig. 3.30): both represent the apogee of Iron Age architecture in Wales – it would have been a hugely daunting prospect for any rival tribe to attempt an assault on such formidable strongholds as these.

Yet despite the varied size and intimidating appearance of the Celtic hillforts, they were ultimately to prove ineffective in withstanding the relentless approach of a ruthless and determined enemy from overseas.

Fig. 3.7 Castell Odo, Aberdaron (SH 187 284). Situated near the tip of the Llŷn Peninsula of North Wales, Castell Odo is a simple bivallate enclosure of Early Iron Age date. Excavation revealed that the slighter outer enclosure was built first, then the stronger inner rampart added at a later date. The irregular surface of the fort retains the outlines of several roundhouses, and also a cigar-shaped earthwork known as a 'Pillow Mound' (an artificial rabbit burrow) indicating that in medieval or later times, the old hillfort was used as a warren to breed rabbits for meat and fur.

Fig. 3.8 Carn Bentyrch, Llangybi (SH 425 417). Just like Castell Odo, this site clearly displays several phases of construction, although in the absence of excavation the exact sequence is uncertain. The small central stone ringwork is much better preserved than the rest of the site and it is likely to be a late addition (it has even been suggested that it was the stronghold of an early-medieval ruler of the region). The ringwork has been built within a more typical hillfort marked by the outer circle of earth and stone, with an inturned entrance just visible towards the right-hand side. There is a third enclosure here, although it is much less prominent and has been overlain by a modern field wall (which preserves its curving line visible in the background). This was perhaps an annexe or stock enclosure adjoining the fort. Carn Bentyrch can be reached by a footpath from the famous holy well beside the church in Llangybi village. This view looks north-west towards the great hillfort of Tre'r Ceiri on the horizon (Fig. 3.31).

Fig. 3.9 Caer Caradog, Cerrigydrudion (SH 967 479). Despite an obscuring covering of snow, the visual evidence suggests this is another two-phase site, the more obvious rampart and ditch enclosing a much less substantial circuit. In this view (looking south across the site), the corduroy pattern of ploughing can just be discerned, suggesting that the feeble inner ring could be a relatively recent agricultural feature. Excavations in 1963–4 unfortunately revealed few defining features. This is one of a number of hillforts named after the famous Celtic warrior Caratacus (*Caradog* in Welsh) who fought against the Romans – though whether this site had any real connection with the historical figure is debatable.

Fig. 3.10 Romans Castle, Milford Haven (SM 895 106). This is another misnamed site, for there is nothing to suggest that the Romans had anything to do with it. This is a classic multivallate Iron Age fort of slightly irregular plan, but well-sited to take advantage of the highest hill in this corner of Pembrokeshire. Two concentric lines of defence are evident in this view (looking towards the west), but there was an additional outer line that has been largely ploughed away and obscured by later hedgerows. Like other hillforts, it is probable that the multiple defences are the result of alterations and additions over a long period of time.

Fig. 3.11 Castell Nadolig, Aberporth (SN 298 504). Centuries of intensive agricultural activity have almost obliterated the low earthworks of this oddly-named site ('Christmas Castle'), but the outline of the widely-spaced bivallate enclosure has been preserved by the overlying hedgerows. The A487 Cardigan to Aberaeron road clips the south side of the fort (right). In 1829 a remarkable discovery was made here – a pair of very rare bronze decorated spoons dating from around 50BC–AD 100. They were almost certainly not made for domestic use, but rather for important rituals and ceremonies, and were donated to the Ashmolean Museum in Oxford, where they can still be seen.

OPPOSITE: **Figs 3.12a** & **3.12b Maendy Camp, Rhondda** (SS 957 956). High above the former mining town of Treorchy lies a modest settlement, defended by concentric drystone walls (now reduced to low grassy banks). Like many sites in the Glamorgan uplands, the defensive lines are widely spaced apart, perhaps to allow sufficient room to corral livestock. The entrances into both enclosures are sharply inturned, perhaps for defensive purposes, but equally to make it easier to herd the animals inside (see reconstruction drawing **3.12b** below). A Bronze Age dagger was discovered here in 1901, but the site is presumed to be of Iron Age or Romano-British date.

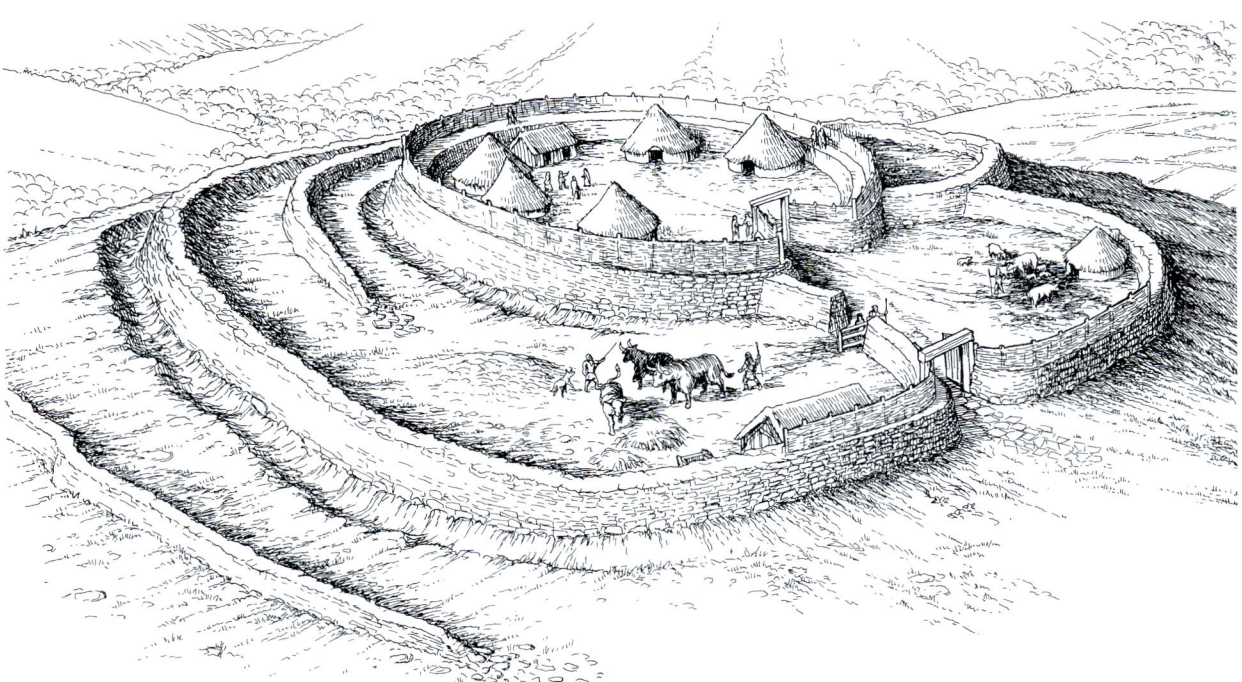

Fig. 3.13a Moel Ton-mawr, Maesteg (SS 825 871). Another upland Glamorgan settlement with widely-spaced defences and a series of annexes or stock enclosures (extending out of view to the left). This well-preserved earthwork is one of five similar sites on the same mountain (see also Fig. 3.5).

LEFT: **Fig. 3.13b Blaen-y-Cwm** is a near-neighbour to Moel Ton-mawr, and an almost identical earthwork comprising a fortified enclosure of angular plan, with a very large outer compound. What is particularly intriguing about this site is that it appears to have been built over the line of the compound ditch, indicating that the fort is a later addition to what was originally an unfortified site.

Fig. 3.14 Foel Faner, Dolgellau (SH 734 204). This univallate enclosure is one of three stone-built hillforts in the uplands north of Dolgellau. The defences consist simply of a stone wall pierced with an entrance gap, enclosing the irregular summit of the hill. Although now reduced to rubble, the wall must have been quite strong when first built, and perhaps stood almost 3m high. Coupled with the lofty location, this little fort must have been a formidably secure retreat for its inhabitants. This view looks east across the site to Llyn Cynwch and the peak of Foel Offrwm, which is crowned by an even larger hillfort.

Fig. 3.15 Pen-y-gaer, Llanidloes (SN 908 868). An almost identical hillfort to Foel Faner, where the builders again opted for a simple, but strong, drystone wall to enclose their settlement. The entrance was a gap on the south-east (right) side. A small stony cairn, presumably of Bronze Age date and therefore predating the hillfort, can be seen near the centre of the enclosure. In the background stretches the expanse of the Llyn Clywedog reservoir, built in the 1960s to regulate the flow of the Severn and to help provide a water supply for the Midlands.

Guard chambers

Fig. 3.16 Carn Alw, Crymych (SN 139 338). This is a strange little fort located on the north-facing slopes of Mynydd Preseli. In this view looking east, a modestly-sized walled enclosure of triangular plan can be seen backing against a natural rock outcrop. As originally planned, the entrance was a simple gap through the middle of the drystone wall, but the builders went to remarkable lengths in order to defend that entrance. Around the more level approach to the south and west is a *chevaux-de-frise* – a pincushion of upright stones set into the ground to deter horse-borne attack or a headlong rush of foot soldiers (arrowed white). Anyone wanting to get inside would be channelled along a walled avenue (arrowed blue), passing a pair of guard chambers on the way. Why were such elaborate defences needed for such a little fort? Was it simply a case of hubris on the part of the occupants, to make their home look far more important than it really was? Or could there have been a greater significance to the location that we can no longer appreciate 2,000 years on? Could it have been a chieftain's personal stronghold rather than a communal refuge, or might it even have been a sacred site connected with Iron Age rituals and beliefs?

Fig. 3.17 Cwm-berwyn, Builth Wells (SO 073 549). The weather can play strange tricks at times. Temperature inversion has caused a sea of fog to form in the valleys around Builth Wells. leaving only the highest peaks of the Radnorshire Carneddau exposed to the feeble warmth of the winter sun. In this view looking north-west, the Cwm-berwyn promontory fort emerges in the foreground, the defensive ramparts marked by two parallel dark lines. Pockmarks within the interior indicate the position of at least six roundhouses.

Fig. 3.18 Pen y Bannau, Pontrhydfendigaid (SN 742 668). This hillfort occupies a dramatic outcrop overlooking the village of Pontrhydfendigaid near Aberystwyth. This view (looking south across the hill) was taken in December 2022 and, despite the heavy covering of snow, the salient features of the site are quite clear. The foreground approach is guarded by three massive ramparts with an entrance path snaking through them, leading through a gap into a relatively small courtyard on the summit. A second enclosure extends beyond the main fort towards the top left of the photo, although this relied mostly on the natural slopes for protection. The massing of defences on just one side shows the direction that an attack might be expected, but the sheer scale of the earthworks is at odds with the size of the enclosed space. No attempt seems to have been made to continue the ramparts around to the left-hand flank, where the slopes are less precipitous. It might therefore be argued that the builders were more concerned in creating a monumental façade to impress anyone approaching the site, rather than an effective defensive perimeter.

Fig. 3.19 Watery Bay, Marloes (SM 768 079). This is one of the most westerly promontory forts in Pembrokeshire. This view is looking west towards the island of Skokholm, with Skomer just visible on the right. The relatively small enclosure is defended by at least two lines of defence, the innermost considered to be a possible addition.

Fig. 3.20 Flimston Bay Camp (SR 930 945). Flimston Bay is arguably the finest of the many promontory forts along this dramatic stretch of the south Pembrokeshire coast. Multiple curving earthworks cut off the only possible approach to the headland, which has been damaged by limestone quarrying and natural erosion over the centuries.

Fig. 3.21 Castell Coch, Trefin (SM 840 338). A classic example of a promontory fort, where a sizeable headland needed just a few short ditches and banks for it to be securely protected from attack. Despite the large area enclosed by the defences (1.7 hectares), there are no obvious signs of any hut circles to be seen. The photo, taken looking due west along the headland, also illustrates the danger posed to coastal archaeology by natural erosion. The isthmus is probably narrower than it would have been in the Iron Age, and the sharply defined cliff edge to the right shows that the headland has been eaten away in fairly recent times. The sea will eventually break through the neck and turn the headland into an island.

Fig. 3.22 Dinas Mawr, Pwllderi
(SM 887 386). Further along the coast on the Pencaer peninsula near Fishguard is a more intriguing fort, quite different in scale and layout to Castell Coch. Here the site is overlooked by higher ground and the two widely-spaced lines of defence enclose small crescents of steeply-sloping land. Since most of the interior is taken up by an enormous boss of rock, it is puzzling why this seemingly unsuitable location was chosen in the first place. Perhaps there was some esoteric reason that we can no longer appreciate, the strange rock being a feature that the Iron Age builders wanted to incorporate into their home.

Fig. 3.23 Caerau, Abereiddy
(SM 788 308). Caerau is a more typical promontory fort on the same stretch of coastline, and also accessible to walkers along the Pembrokeshire Coast Path. Here the almost circular living area is defended by multiple banks and ditches, pointing to several phases of construction. Just out of shot to the east (right) is another promontory fort, a much smaller site with just a single rampart and ditch. The relationship between the two sites is puzzling: were they built at different periods or were they contemporary? If the latter, were they perhaps inhabited by people of differing social status, or did they have completely separate functions?

These three hillforts near Brecon demonstrate the various ways in which Iron Age builders adapted the landscape to suit their needs.

Fig. 3.24 Crug Hywel (SO 225 206) is a prominent tabletop peak overlooking Crickhowell in the Usk valley. The summit has been scarped on all sides in order to render the teardrop-shaped enclosure even more secure.

Fig. 3.25 Gaer Fawr (SO 021 380) is at Upper Chapel, and is an inland promontory fort with massive defences heaped only on the more vulnerable approach, leaving the natural slopes to protect the remaining sides.

Fig. 3.26 Twyn-y-gaer (SO 053 353) is an oddly-shaped odd site of, looking like a giant green lolly pop or a tank turret. The rounded enclosure is a typical univallate fort, but the layout has been confused by the long earthwork extending out from the entrance. In all likelihood this is a much later 'pillow mound', added when the fort interior may have been used as a rabbit warren.

Fig. 3.27 Cefn-y-castell, Trewern
(SJ 305 134). This fine fort, accessible
by a stiff climb up from the A458, is
located on Middletown Hill, last bastion
of upland Wales before the Shropshire
plains are reached. The massive
rampart and slight outer ditch encloses
an uneven and elongated summit
that incorporates a much older burial
cairn. There were gates into the fort
at either end, having deeply inturned
entrances, which were designed to
increase the obstacles facing any
attacker (as if the climb itself wasn't a
sufficient deterrent). This view shows
the north-east gate prominently in the
foreground.

Fig. 3.28 Castle Bank, Hundred House
(SO 087 561). A number of hillforts
exist in the uplands between Builth
Wells and New Radnor, and this is the
most impressive of them. It is set on
a high rocky ridge that offered good
natural protection and a commanding
view, but forced the builders to opt for
an exceptionally elongated layout. The
stone-walled fort is just 84m wide at
most, but 290m in length, and there is an
outer enclosure (extending out of shot
to the left), so that the whole site is over
400m long. Shadowy pockmarks indicate
the site of numerous roundhouses within
the enclosure. This view looks north
over the main fort, with the deeply-
inturned entrance in the foreground
(the circular features in the rubble are
modern shelters).

Fig. 3.29 Foeldrygarn, Crymych (SN 157 336). One of the major Iron Age sites of Wales, Foeldrygarn ('the hill of three cairns') lies on the eastern edge of Mynydd Preseli. The burial mounds that give the place its name are particularly obvious in this view, which looks south-west across the hill. They predate the fort by 1,000 or more years, and their good state of preservation shows that they were retained and respected by the Iron Age builders. Two circuits of stony ramparts can also be seen, and there is a third wall defining an annexe out of shot to the left. Also visible are the numerous pockmarks of vanished roundhouses (227 is a conservative estimate) indicating that this was a major tribal settlement and stronghold during Iron Age and Romano-British times.

Fig. 3.30 Pen-y-crug, Brecon (SO 029 304). This is one of the most impressive multivallate hillforts in Wales. The sinuous and sculptural quality of the earthworks are well appreciated in this view, taken from the north and looking towards the backdrop of the Bannau Brycheiniog (Brecon Beacons). The defences comprise up to five ramparts closely hugging the contours around the summit enclosure. Despite its appearance as an earthwork, it is thought that the inner two circuits, at the least, had stone revetments or walling. The entrance into the fort was on the south side (furthest from the camera) where there was a small annexe (visible in Fig. 3.2), although that side has unfortunately been damaged by later quarries and is now very overgrown. Despite the scale of the defences and the effort involved in its construction, there are no obvious signs of any hut circles within the interior; but since the hilltop has been subjected to ploughing in relatively modern times, it may be that any surface features have been obliterated.

PREVIOUS PAGE AND THIS SPREAD: **Figs 3.31a, 3.31b** & **3.31c Tre'r Ceiri, Llanaelhaearn** (SH 374 447). Another site of superlatives, Tre'r Ceiri is arguably the most impressive and formidable monument of the Celtic Iron Age surviving in Wales, and careful restoration in the 1990s has only added to its grandeur. It is hardly surprising that this was once thought to be the home of giants (as the place-name translates). The fort crowns one of the high peaks that dominate this corner of the Llŷn Peninsula, and can be accessed by a steep path from the B4417. The abundant scree was used to build a single massive drystone wall up to 3.5m high, enclosing the elongated and irregular peak. A slighter wall defended the marginally less precipitous north-west flank. On the very summit is a large Bronze Age cairn that was retained by the fort builders out of respect for their predecessors.

ABOVE: There were two main gates into the fort, narrow tunnel-like passages that restricted the number of people entering at any one time, but there were also three other postern gates, through which the defenders could sneak out to launch a counter-attack, or make a quick getaway if things turned sour. One of them is still roofed over with massive slabs. On the lower slopes of the hill, half hidden by heather and scree, are numerous walled enclosures and platforms (perhaps used by the occupants as vegetable plots or animal pens). Within the fort itself are over 150 stone hut sites. Careful study of the remains suggest that originally there were only about 26 large roundhouses here, and that at a later date they were modified and supplemented by the addition of numerous smaller huts of sub-rectangular plan. Pottery of second-century date has been found, pointing to renewed occupation of the fort by native inhabitants well into Roman times.

OPPOSITE: The monumental scale of Tre'r Ceiri and its dominating position in the landscape can well be appreciated in this view, looking north-east across the fort to the misty peaks of Eryri.

Fig. 3.32 Pentre Camp, Llanfair Caereinion (SJ 118 096). Not all Iron Age forts are as well-preserved as those shown in preceding pages; many have been obliterated by centuries of agricultural ploughing, while here are two sites that have been worn down to such an extent that the feeble earthworks only show up as shadows when the sun is particularly low. Pentre Camp would have been a very impressive sight originally, with no less than five defensive rings encircling the small hilltop like a tiered wedding cake. This view from the east clearly shows the entrance passage leading up to the innermost enclosure.

Fig. 3.33 Coed-y-caerau, Newport (ST 379 917). Here again, a very low winter sun has helped illuminate the curious earthworks on Kemeys Hill near Newport. This view looks west over the Usk Valley. There are three sites in a line here, practically overlapping each other – a circular univallate enclosure at the top left, then a bivallate enclosure with concentric defences in the middle and finally the rectangular earthwork with rounded corners in the foreground. This is probably a multiperiod site, and the rectangular earthwork has every appearance of being a Roman fortlet, perhaps set up here to keep an eye on the locals (the legionary base at Caerleon, opposite and Fig. 4.10, is only a short distance away).

OPPOSITE: The excavated remains of the Roman amphitheatre at Caerleon

ROMAN WALES

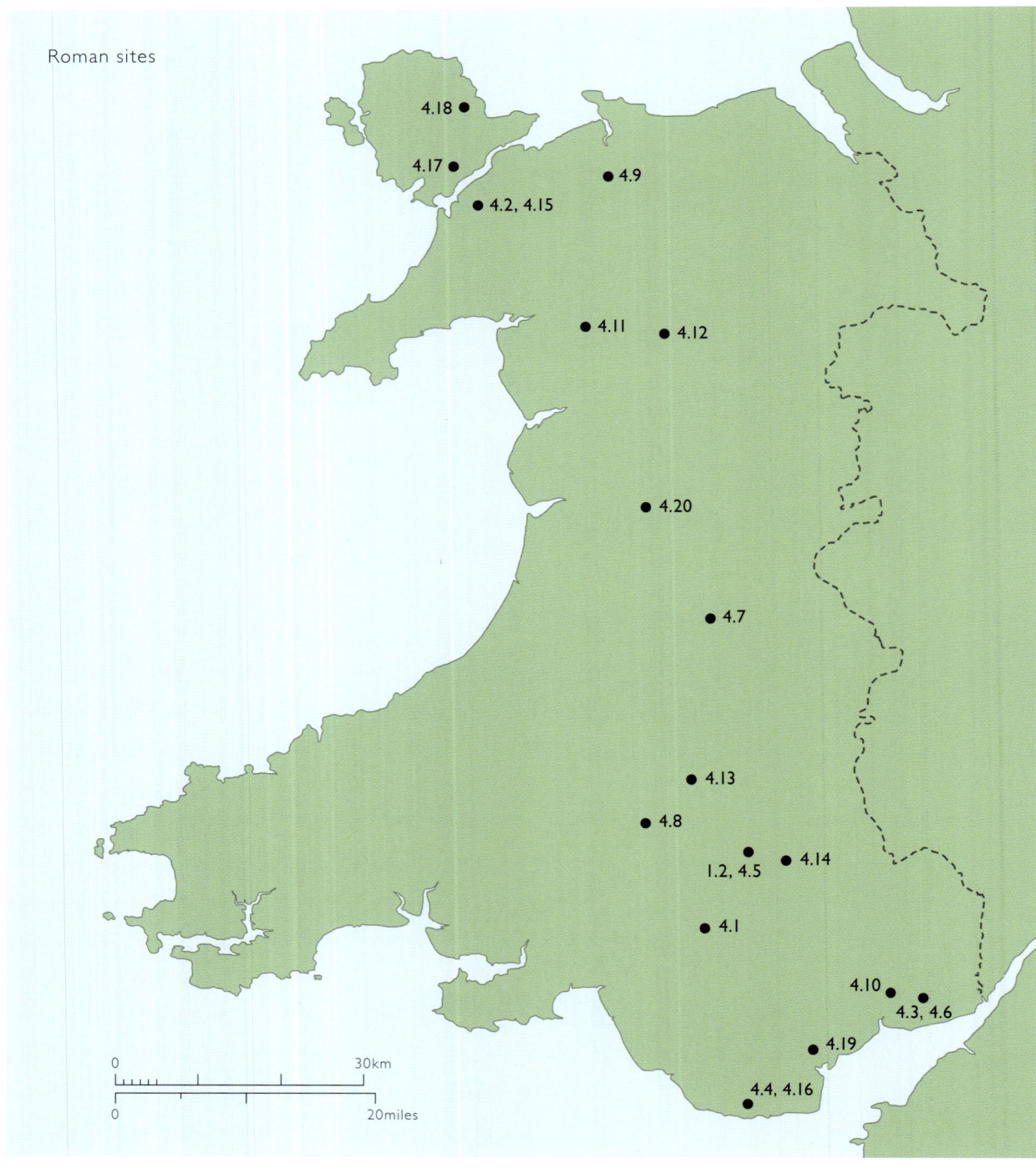

Roman sites

4.18 ●

4.17 ●

4.2, 4.15 ●

● 4.9

● 4.11   ● 4.12

● 4.20

● 4.7

● 4.13

● 4.8

● 4.14
1.2, 4.5 ●

● 4.1

4.10 ●   ● 4.3, 4.6

● 4.19

4.4, 4.16 ●

0 ⊢⊢⊢⊢⊢⊢⊢⊢⊣ 30km

0 ⊢⊢⊢⊢⊢⊢⊢⊢⊣ 20miles

4.

THE MOST EFFICIENT and ruthless military organisation in the ancient world made its presence felt in Wales in the first century AD, in the course of a campaign to bring Britain under the sway of Rome. Julius Caesar had made exploratory landings in 55–54BC, but it was not until the reign of Emperor Claudius a century later that a full-blooded invasion took place. In AD 43 the Roman war-machine landed on the Kent shore with four legions of heavily-armed and rigorously drilled soldiers, along with auxiliary troops and supporting cavalry (some 40,000 in all). The Celtic warriors of southern and eastern Britain were soon cowed by the discipline and military superiority of the Roman army, their tribal hillforts falling one by one to the invaders; but the conquest of Wales, which began in about AD 48, was a far more protracted and bloody undertaking due to the rugged terrain and fierce resistance from the native tribes. The names of some of these tribes are recorded by Roman writers, and we know that at the forefront of the resistance were the *Silures* in the south, and the *Ordovices* and *Deceangli* in the north. For a time, they were led by Caratacus, a warrior of the Catuvellauni tribe of south-east England, who had been ousted by

the advancing Romans and retreated westwards to continue the fight. Caratacus was defeated in battle somewhere in mid Wales in AD 51 and was taken in chains to Rome, where his proudly defiant stance before the emperor at least saved his life, if not his liberty.

His capture did not end resistance to Roman rule, and further bloody campaigns were launched. Stronghold of the resistance was the island of Anglesey, and the historian Tacitus paints a vivid picture of the ferocious attack that took place there in about AD 60. The soldiers were at first terrified by the spectacle of armed warriors, frenzied women and cursing Druids lining the shore of the Menai Strait, but in the end military discipline won through and they plunged into battle to wreak the usual sanguinary havoc. But the impetus of conquest faltered as troops were hurriedly withdrawn to deal with a revolt in the east, led by the warrior queen Boudicca.

It was not until AD 74, after a period of civil war in Rome following the death of Nero, and the appearance of a new Flavian dynasty of emperors, that a more concerted effort was undertaken against the native tribes. To accomplish this task, the newly-appointed military governor Julius Frontinus established a huge new legionary fortress at Chester (*Deva*) in the north, and another in the south at Caerleon (*Isca*). The vast 50-acre encampment at Caerleon (Fig. 4.10) on the banks of the Usk became the headquarters of the Second Augustan Legion, one of only three legions permanently garrisoned in Britain. The fort held around 5,500 men, and in time was provided with a magnificent amphitheatre and extensive quayside buildings to deal with all the ships bringing supplies and goods from the Continent and the Mediterranean.

Fig. 4.1 A Roman road known as Sarn Helen, now marked by a grassy track, crosses the mountains between the forts at Neath and Brecon

Both Caerleon and Chester served as hubs to at least 30 auxiliary forts and military stations. (Auxiliaries – from the Latin *auxilia*, meaning 'helpers' – were not Roman citizens but volunteers recruited from occupied territories outside Italy. After serving for 25 years, the auxiliary soldier would be awarded citizenship and could retire from the army.) These auxiliary forts included Brecon (Fig. 4.5), Caerhun (Fig. 4.9) and Caernarfon (Fig. 4.15), which were all strategically positioned about a day's march apart and linked by a network of roads. These roads were surveyed and built in arrow-straight sections cleared of any encroaching forestry, to deny any cover for an enemy ambush, and enable the rapid deployment of troops. Some are still in use today, having been utilised by newer forms of traffic over the centuries, while others were abandoned, preserved only as footpaths, field boundaries or faint earthworks (Fig. 4.1).

The geometric regularity that characterises Roman military and civilian works makes them very easy to spot from the air, and the discovery of any large, right-angled enclosure is usually a good indication that it belongs to the Romano-British period. The curvilinear forms that had predominated in the Bronze and Iron Ages, and which utilised the irregularities of the ground to best advantage, gave way to orderly lines plotted out by Roman surveyors, stamping their mark on the landscape with rigid disregard for the existing topography. Forts were almost universally built to a rectangular plan with rounded corners (commonly referred to as 'playing card' shape). The fort defences were initially constructed from earth

Fig. 4.2 Part of the excavated bath house at *Segontium* (Caernarfon)

and timber, and comprised a series of outer ditches with a steep turf rampart topped with wooden stockades and watch-towers. Each side of the fort had a gateway giving access to the interior, which was divided up by a series of roads into a chessboard pattern of blocks (*insulae*) in which would be built barracks, workshops and stores. Near the centre of the compound stood two important buildings – the fort headquarters (*principia*) and the commander's residence (*praetorium*). The initial buildings were quickly and cheaply built from timber, set on stone footings to keep the wood from rotting, but in subsequent years the more important and strategic sites were rebuilt in durable masonry.

An important facet of Mediterranean life introduced by the Romans into Britain was the bath house. It would have been unthinkable for a fort, town or a grand country house, not to have such a facility, as bathing was considered to be very much a part of civilised society. The legionary fortress at Caerleon was big enough to have two: one inside the perimeter (which has been preserved for viewing), and another just outside. A typical bath house featured a series of chambers through which the patron progressed, from the initial disrobing room (*apodyterium*) to the warm room (*tepidarium*) and then finally the hot room (*caldarium*). The whole process was designed to make the patron sweat, so that servants could massage scented oil into the skin and remove the slimy residue with a skilful sweep of a blunt metal blade. A quick dip in the plunge pool of the cold room (*frigidarium*) would close up the pores. It must have been a far more enjoyable process than it sounds. The bath house was intended to be a place to socialise, as well as to keep clean (though just how hygienic these places actually were is debatable).

Fig. 4.3 The pillars of a hypocaust system at Caerwent

The power behind this process was another Roman import, a cleverly designed underfloor heating system (*hypocaust*). This consisted of a stone surface raised on pillars, so that hot air from an adjacent furnace could circulate through the void and warm up the floor above (Fig. 4.3). The rising heat was also channelled through ceramic ducts embedded in the walls for an extra bit of warmth. Water was supplied to the fort along a pipe or leat from a nearby spring or stream, and would then have been used to flush the latrines and channel the waste away. Out beyond the gates of the fort a shanty town usually grew up. This was known as a *vicus*, and would have been occupied by retired veterans, soldiers' families and local traders hoping to cash in on the hard-earned wages of the troops. Such garrison settlements had the potential to develop into more permanent establishments, but in Wales they had a very precarious existence and depended entirely on the success of the fort. The withdrawal of troops to fight elsewhere on the frontier would have had a major impact on the life of the inhabitants and their businesses.

While on campaign, the troops were kept in shape and ready for action by carrying out military exercises, which included the building of miniature forts known as 'practice camps'. These are often found in large numbers close to an established military base – 15 or so survive at Tomen y Mur near Trawsfynydd, while around 20 have been recorded on Llandrindod Common south of the town, built by troops from the nearby fort at Castell Collen. Even when on the move, soldiers would be expected to ensure that their overnight halt was sufficiently protected against attack, by quickly building a 'marching camp'.

Once the site for the halt was decided upon, surveyors would mark out the limits of the camp and each soldier would be allocated a section of ditch to dig and a length of rampart to be heaped up from the resultant spoil. This was topped with a line of wooden spears (two being carried by every soldier as part of his kit). The four entrances into the camp were protected against surprise attacks by either a detached section of bank and ditch set in front of the gap, or by an inwardly curving passageway (*clavicula*), both of which were designed to prevent a forward rush and to force an enemy to expose his flank to the defenders. Within the protective enclave, troops would arrange their leather tents in rows much like the layout of the permanent forts. Smaller eight-man tents for the rank and file, while larger, more elaborate tents were set up for the officers. During the night some troops would be resting, while others would take their turn on guard duty. In the morning, the whole camp would be dismantled before the army marched away.

Because of their impermanence, marching camps do not survive as well as other Roman fortifications, and can often be very difficult to spot from the ground. However, from the air they are more apparent, and their sheer size indicates the huge number of men involved in construction. One of the best-preserved sites in Wales is Y Pigwn (Fig. 4.8) on the high moors between Trecastle and Llandovery. There are actually two camps here, one superimposed upon the other. The larger and earlier camp enclosed just over 37 acres of land and would have accommodated around 5,000 men, while the second was of approximately 25 acres in extent and housed about 4,000 troops. That two separate camps should be built on the same site (rather than just reusing the older defences), is probably down to the strictly regimented military mind; though why they should be skewed is less easy to understand – did the second gang of surveyors simply get it wrong?

For almost 40 years, Wales was little more than a turbulent frontier zone. Julius Frontinus was succeeded by an even more belligerent tactician, Julius Agricola (governor from AD 78 to 85), who defeated the *Ordovices* of North Wales before heading north to deal with the Scots. Once the bitter business of subjugation was accomplished, the Roman administrators sought to encourage trade amongst the natives and a dependence on their civilised way of life, while at the same time exploiting the mineral wealth of the country. This may have been the main reason why Britain was invaded in the first place. Advanced Roman technology was used to extract copper, lead, silver and gold from deposits in the Welsh hills.

But in contrast to the numerous towns and cities that the Romans established in England, only two urban centres were ever planned in Wales – Carmarthen (*Moridunum*) and Caerwent (*Venta Silurum*). Of the former, nothing survives above ground, although the rectangular outline is reflected in the layout of modern streets, but much more remains to be seen at Caerwent (Fig. 4.6). The Roman name means 'market town of the Silures', for it was established as a regional capital for the humbled Silures, who were encouraged to leave their war-torn hillforts and live a civilised Roman existence in the valley below. At first just a collection of buildings lining an east-west road, it developed into a walled city of grand stone buildings, with an estimated population of 3,000 at its height. Unlike nearby Caerleon, Caerwent still retains a largely rural setting today, and many of the undisturbed Roman foundations have been excavated and preserved. These include the remains of street-front shops, a temple and part of the forum-basilica complex (the chief civic buildings of Roman urban life). The forum was a large open market square surrounded on three sides by colonnaded shops and offices, while the fourth side of the piazza was occupied by the basilica, a grand aisled building serving as the main administrative centre or town hall. Some of the buildings in Caerwent had the ultimate in imported luxuries, an underfloor heating system, though less affluent homeowners had to make do with a hearth or portable brazier to keep the chill Welsh weather at bay.

Elsewhere in the countryside, Roman-style farmsteads and villas were built by affluent landowners who had embraced the benefits offered by the Mediterranean way of life. Admittedly, with a very few exceptions, the Welsh villas were never as lavish or as extensive as those built in lowland England. They occur mostly in the richer agricultural lands of Glamorgan, Monmouth and Pembrokeshire, areas where the native Celts seem to have adopted Roman ways far more readily than their countrymen in the mountainous north. The

largest and most elaborate villa so far discovered stood at Llantwit Major in the Vale of Glamorgan, which has been periodically excavated between 1887 and 1978. Archaeologists have uncovered the foundations of stone buildings of varying sizes grouped around two courtyards. The complex developed over time, and reached its greatest extent between AD *c.*270 and 350. The main residential north wing comprised an L-shaped arrangement of small box-like chambers linked by a covered veranda along the frontage. Some rooms had mosaic floors, plastered and painted walls, glazed windows and partial underfloor heating. There was even a bath suite at one end of the range (Fig. 4.4). More recent geophysical surveys have revealed a complex sequence of ditches and boundary banks surrounding the buildings. After the excavations had finished the foundations of the villa were covered over, so all that can now be seen is a rather shapeless earthwork in a field (Fig. 4.16).

More recent archaeological investigations between 2009 and 2015 have revealed the site of a modest villa at Abermagwr, in a remote area of Ceredigion, which had been noted as a cropmark back in 1979. Believed to be occupied between AD 250 and 350, it was a relatively simple block incorporating cross-wings and a veranda, and stood within a large, ditched enclosure. Though lacking mosaic floors and hypocaust heating, its Romano-British owner was clearly wealthy enough to afford luxury glassware and a roof of decorative slates. Aerial photography has identified the cropmarks of similar winged villas in other parts of South Wales, which await proper exploration at a future date.

In contrast to these fine stone constructions, most rural farmsteads of the Romano-British period appear to have been fairly humble structures,

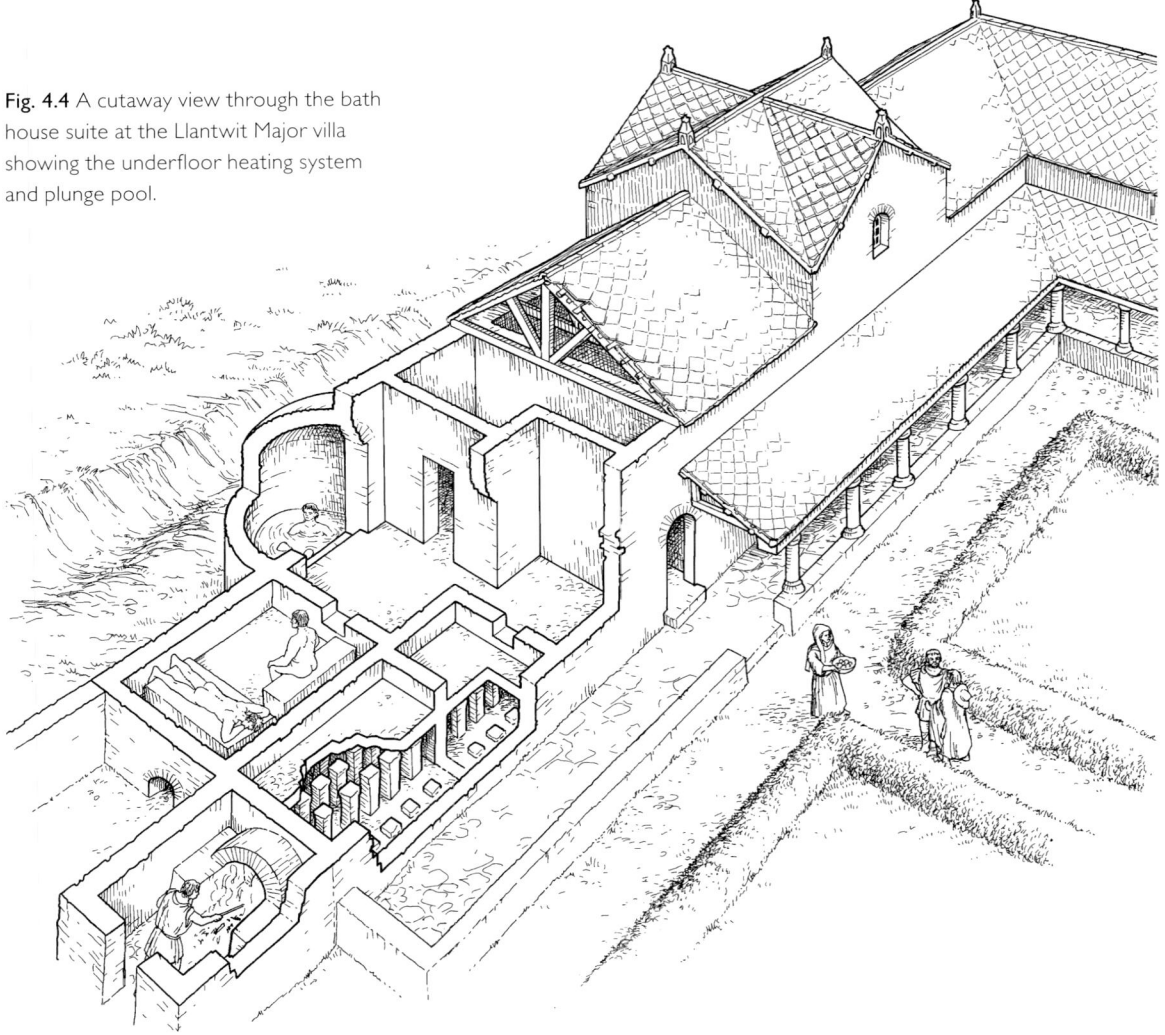

Fig. 4.4 A cutaway view through the bath house suite at the Llantwit Major villa showing the underfloor heating system and plunge pool.

hardly different from the roundhouse settlements of the preceding Bronze and Iron Ages, though they sometimes feature the innovative rectangular buildings favoured by the Romans. Two good examples can be visited on Anglesey: the double-banked earthwork enclosure of Caer Lêb (Fig. 4.17) and the stone-walled hut group at Din Lligwy (Fig. 4.18). There is evidence that some Iron Age hillforts remained in occupation, though whether they were allowed to be maintained as defensible strongholds seems less likely.

During the third and fourth centuries a series of political upheavals signalled a long, slow decline of Roman authority in Britain. There were periods of vicious civil war as short-lived usurpers redeployed troops from embattled front lines to bolster their own bids for power. Punitive retaliation would bring some measure of stability, but then another warmonger would shatter the enforced peace. The situation was made worse by increasing pirate raids from Saxons, Irish and Scots, stretching the resources of the far-flung Empire to breaking point. Coastal defences were upgraded to combat the menace. Around AD 300 a substantial stone fort of 9-acre extent was built at Cardiff (Fig. 4.19), a westerly outlier of a defensive chain that had been established to guard the south-west coastline of Britain against Saxon incursions. The earth and timber defences of Caerwent were replaced with masonry around the same time, and several decades afterwards multangular bastions and outer ditches were added as an extra precaution. New stone-walled fortlets were also built at Caernarfon and Holyhead.

These late works were probably intended to protect shipping and act as bases for counter-attacks against the pirates, but they might equally have been built by breakaway emperors to guard against retaliation from Rome itself. The most notable of these rival rulers was Magnus Maximus, Roman general of Britain who, in AD 383, successfully usurped the imperial diadem and ruled the western empire for the next five years. He appears in Welsh mythology as Macsen Wledig, and is also credited with being the founder of later Welsh royal dynasties. According to the sixth-century historian Gildas, Magnus was responsible for withdrawing all the troops from Britain to campaign in Gaul, never to return. While this is probably an exaggeration (there is evidence that some military bases continued to operate in a reduced capacity for some years afterwards), this period probably saw the effective end of the Roman military presence in Wales and western parts of Britain. The final break

took place in AD 410 when the current emperor, struggling and failing to hold back the tide of Germanic invaders from the gates of Rome itself, officially told the civic leaders of Britain that they must fend for themselves.

OPPOSITE: **Figs 4.5a, 4.5b** & **4.5c Y Gaer, Brecon** (SO 003 297). Y Gaer was one of a string of auxiliary forts established around the heartland of the troublesome *Silures*. The initial timber fort probably dates to around AD 75–80 and was one of the largest in Wales. The defences were rebuilt in stone around AD 140 and there are hints that the walls were repaired in late- or even post-Roman times. The photo opposite (bottom left, **Fig. 4.5b**) also shows the recently conserved remains of the west gate, a typical design comprising a pair of arched carriageways flanked by rectangular guardrooms, which (less typically) project well forward of the gate. The drawing (**Fig. 4.5c**) shows how the gate may have originally looked.

ABOVE: **Fig. 4.6 Caerwent Roman town** (ST 469 905). The town of *Venta Silurum* was founded once the Silures had been ruthlessly pacified, and during the reign of Emperor Hadrian (AD 117–38) was developed into a major urban centre with shops, houses and civic buildings. A stone wall was built in the late third century to replace the earlier defensive earthworks, although the projecting bastions (just visible in the photo above) were added much later as a precaution against the threat of pirate raids. This view shows Caerwent looking north-east, with the medieval church of St Stephen and St Tathan prominent in the centre.

Fig. 4.7 Roman marching camp at Esgair Perfedd, Rhayader (SN 924 698). This remotely sited temporary camp is one of the best preserved in Wales, though it has been damaged by modern trackways snaking through the interior. This photo was taken on a late January afternoon looking towards the south-east, and clearly shows three sides of the classic playing card outline of the camp, which was defended by an earth rampart and outer ditch. The fourth (further) side is less well-preserved, and beyond it the town of Rhayader and the Wye Valley are hidden by low-lying fog.

Figs 4.8a & 4.8b Marching camps at Y Pigwn, Trecastle (SN 828 313). The above view shows the two superimposed temporary camps looking north-east over the moors towards the Usk Valley. The camps were built on two separate occasions as overnight halts during the initial invasion of Wales, though why the earthworks should be so obviously skewed is very puzzling. The photo (left) shows the divergent ramparts at the north-east corner. In the foreground can be seen one of the *claviculae* or inturned entrances, that would hamper a direct assault on the gate.

Fig. 4.9 Caerhun Roman fort, Conwy (SH 776 704). The characteristic playing card shape of this fort, known as *Canovium*, is clear in this view, taken on a late winter's afternoon looking south. First built around AD 75 in timber, the bank and ditch defences were later reconstructed in stone around AD 140, hence the well-preserved outline under the soil. There were additional buildings outside the gates of the fort, including a *vicus*, a bath house and a dock for supply ships using the tidal River Conwy. Like a number of other forts, the site was reused in medieval times when the parish church of St Mary was built in one corner.

Fig. 4.10a Caerleon, Newport
(SO 340 904). The magnificent
oval amphitheatre now forms the
most striking part of the legionary
fortress of *Isca*. It stood just outside
the fort (the wall is visible in the
background) and was built c.AD
90. The lower part was earth
reinforced with masonry, while the
tiered upper seating was built from
timber. It could house up to 6,000
spectators and was probably used
for military training and gladiatorial
displays. It may also have witnessed
the blood sports and savage
executions that took place in other
arenas across the Empire. Before
excavations started in 1926 only a
grassy hollow could be seen, which
was long fabled to be King Arthur's
Round Table.

Fig. 4.10b Caerleon, Newport
(SO 340 904). At Prysg Field in
the north-west corner of the fort,
excavations and consolidation work
have laid bare the foundations of
typical legionary barrack blocks,
each housing a 'century' (originally
comprising 100 men, although
by the time *Isca* was founded the
number had dropped to 80). Each
century was divided into 10 groups
of 8 men, each group sharing a pair
of the small box-like rooms seen
here. The more spacious suite
of rooms in the foreground was
reserved for the centurion in charge
of his unit. Other buildings visible
in the photo include a latrine block,
a corner turret and faint circular
outlines of cooking ovens.

Fig. 4.11 Tomen y Mur, Trawsfynydd (SH 705 387). This is justly considered to be the best-preserved Roman military landscape in Wales. In this view, looking north towards the mountains of Eryri, the rectangular outline of the fort itself is very obvious, but the surrounding landscape also preserves the remains of roads, practice camps, marching camps, burial mounds, a bath house, an aqueduct and a small amphitheatre. The initial timber fort was probably built in the AD 70s as part of the campaign against the northern tribes, and was reconstructed in stone on a slightly smaller size around AD 140. Although the Roman masonry has been largely robbed away or covered in earth, a small section has been rebuilt to give an impression of the original defences. The prominent mound inside the fort is the remains of a twelfth-century motte castle, probably the one that King William II is recorded as building 'at Mur Castle' in 1095. Even then the old fort was a significant feature of the local landscape, and also makes an appearance in the Welsh folktales *The Mabinogion*.

Fig. 4.12 Caer Gai, Bala (SH 877 316). This fort was established around AD 75 on a hill at the southern end of Llyn Tegid, visible in the background here, looking eastwards. The fort was surrounded by various buildings including a bath house, a guest house, a *vicus* and cemetery. Excavations have identified three phases of defensive work: the original earth and timber rampart, followed by a stone wall, then another earthwork possibly cast up in post-Roman times. In legend, it was the seat of the Arthurian knight Cai (or Kay), but historically was the home of the Vaughans, an important local gentry family, who repaired the old defences for use as a walled garden.

Fig. 4.13 Caerau fort, Beulah (SN 924 503). While post-medieval landscaping has preserved the outlines of Caer Gai, here at Beulah the abandoned fort was returned to farmland, and now only survives as low earthworks, here seen as a rectangular shadow in front of the modern farm buildings. As usual this started out as a timber fort of around AD 75 and was later reduced in size before being abandoned around AD 120, never having been rebuilt in masonry like some other sites. A castle mound in trees behind the farm shows again how the old forts proved attractive to a later breed of invaders.

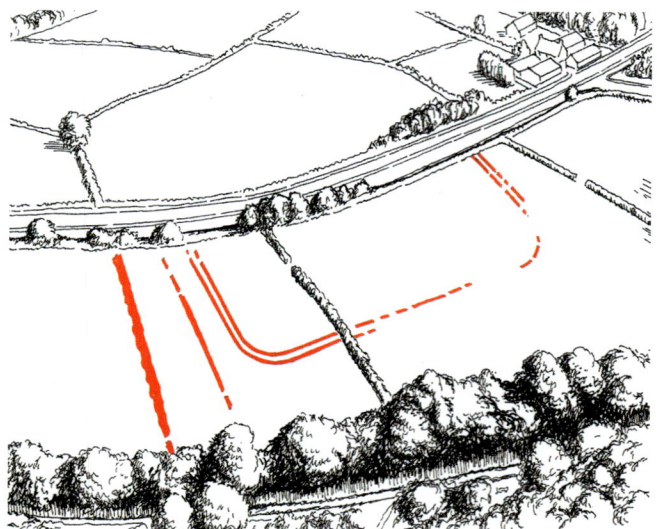

Figs 4.14a & 4.14b Cefn-Brynich fort, Brecon (SO 075 273). Nothing remains above ground of this vanished fort and it was only identified as recently as 2013 during aerial reconnaissance by the RCAHMW. Some clues to its presence had been suggested by the discovery of coins dating to c.AD 43–68, pointing to Roman activity in this area during the earliest phase of the campaign to subdue Wales. In this view, taken in the August heatwave of 2022, a parallel line of ditches appears in the left-hand field, curving around the south-west corner of the fort, before becoming obscured by agricultural marks in the right-hand field. Linear ditches on the left appear to mark additional defences or an annexe. The rest of the fort lies deeply buried in the field to the north, beyond the line of the A40. The drawing shows the basic outline in red of the parchmarks just visible in the photo.

Fig. 4.15 **Segontium Roman fort, Caernarfon** (SH 487 622). Despite the encroachment of modern housing and the A4085 cutting obliquely through the site, the outline of the fort is still clear in this north-westerly view, with the Menai Strait and Anglesey in the background. It was founded c.AD 77 as a base for 1,000 auxiliary infantry, to secure the region after a bitter war against the *Ordovices* of North Wales. The troops were later reduced in number, and from about AD 140 the timber defences were rebuilt in stone. Coins dating from AD 394 suggest this was one of the last forts to be occupied by the Romans in Wales. Among the excavated buildings on display are several barrack blocks, a fine courtyard house for the commander and a small bath house (see also close-up Fig. 4.2). A number of legends and myths have grown up about Segontium, and in *The Mabinogion* it appears as the fabled court of Emperor Maxen. Such beliefs probably inspired King Edward I of England to build an elaborate castle nearby, that deliberately evoked the architectural splendours of imperial Rome (Fig. 6.50).

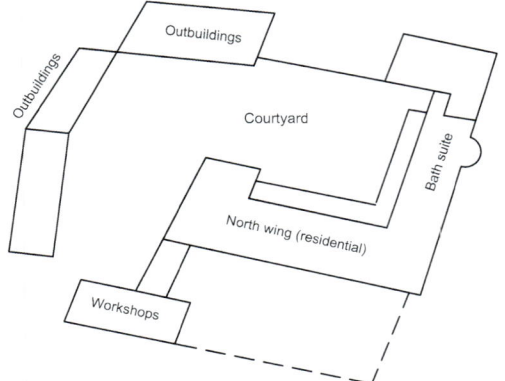

Figs 4.16a & 4.16b Roman villa, Llantwit Major (SS 958 699). Despite having been reburied after several excavations, the stone walls of the villa can still be detected in this view, taken from the north, with a simplified plan (left) adjusted to the same angle. Geophysical surveys in 2016 revealed a series of hidden earthworks, indicating that the more obvious walls were just one part of a complex site. It probably originated as a Late Iron Age farmstead and grew into a very luxurious residence (for this part of Roman Britain at least). The villa reached its maximum prosperity and size by about AD 350 by which time it had grand stone buildings with painted walls, mosaic floors and a bath suite (see also Fig. 4.4). After it was abandoned, the decaying building was used as a burial site, and there is a tradition that it was linked to the Early Christian centre established at Llantwit by St Illtud around AD 500.

The plan (Fig 4.16a) is labelled: Outbuildings; Outbuildings; Courtyard; Bath suite; North wing (residential); Workshops.

Fig. 4.17 Caer Lêb, Brynsiencyn (SH 473 674). The name means 'wet fort', a reference to the unusual low-lying setting of this earthwork and the flooded moats that once surrounded it. The pentagonal bank and ditched enclosure (an additional outer bank has largely disappeared) once sheltered a Romano-British farmstead during the third century AD. Remains of a round hut and square building were found in the courtyard during excavations here in 1866. However, the site could well have originated in the Iron Age, and finds suggest that it may have been reused in medieval times.

Fig. 4.18 Din Lligwy, Moelfre (SH 497 862). This is another Romano-British Anglesey farmstead, occupied during the late-third and early-fourth century AD, and clearly influenced by Roman architecture, with its mix of round and rectangular buildings. The walls were constructed from large slabs of locally quarried limestone, forming a pentagonal enclosure. This is an exceptionally fine monument thanks to restoration following excavation in 1903–7, and is representative of the many enclosed courtyard settlements that can be found by any enthusiastic rambler in the uplands of Gwynedd.

Fig. 4.19 Cardiff Castle, Cardiff (ST 181 766). Despite all the modernity around it, the castle remains the most striking feature of the city centre, here seen from the north-west. It was built around AD 290 to strengthen the coastal defences of Roman Britain, on a site previously occupied by a succession of timber forts. The prominent rectangle of walls and multangular towers are the result of restoration work in the 1920s and are now much higher than they would have been originally. In medieval times the fort was reused as a major castle, of which the great mound and shell-keep are particularly obvious relics.

Fig. 4.20 Penycrocbren fortlet, Dylife (SN 855 934). Not all Roman military works were as monumental as Cardiff Castle. Here, beside the old drovers' track crossing the uplands between Llanidloes and Machynlleth, is a small turf-walled enclosure 25m across. Excavation in 1960 found no obvious evidence of any internal buildings (though they could have been of lightweight timber construction) but there was a strong wooden gate-tower at the north-facing entrance (right in the photo). Similar sites have been noted elsewhere in Wales, and have been compared to the small and lightly manned 'milecastles' of Hadrian's Wall. One suggestion is that it was an outpost to oversee metal mining in the locality. Incidentally, the place-name 'gallows hill' refers to a nearby gibbet where the body of a local murderer was left dangling in the early-1700s.

OPPOSITE: The snow-covered earthworks of Castell Crugerydd in the Radnorshire hills

The Early Medieval period
(AD *c*.410–1100)

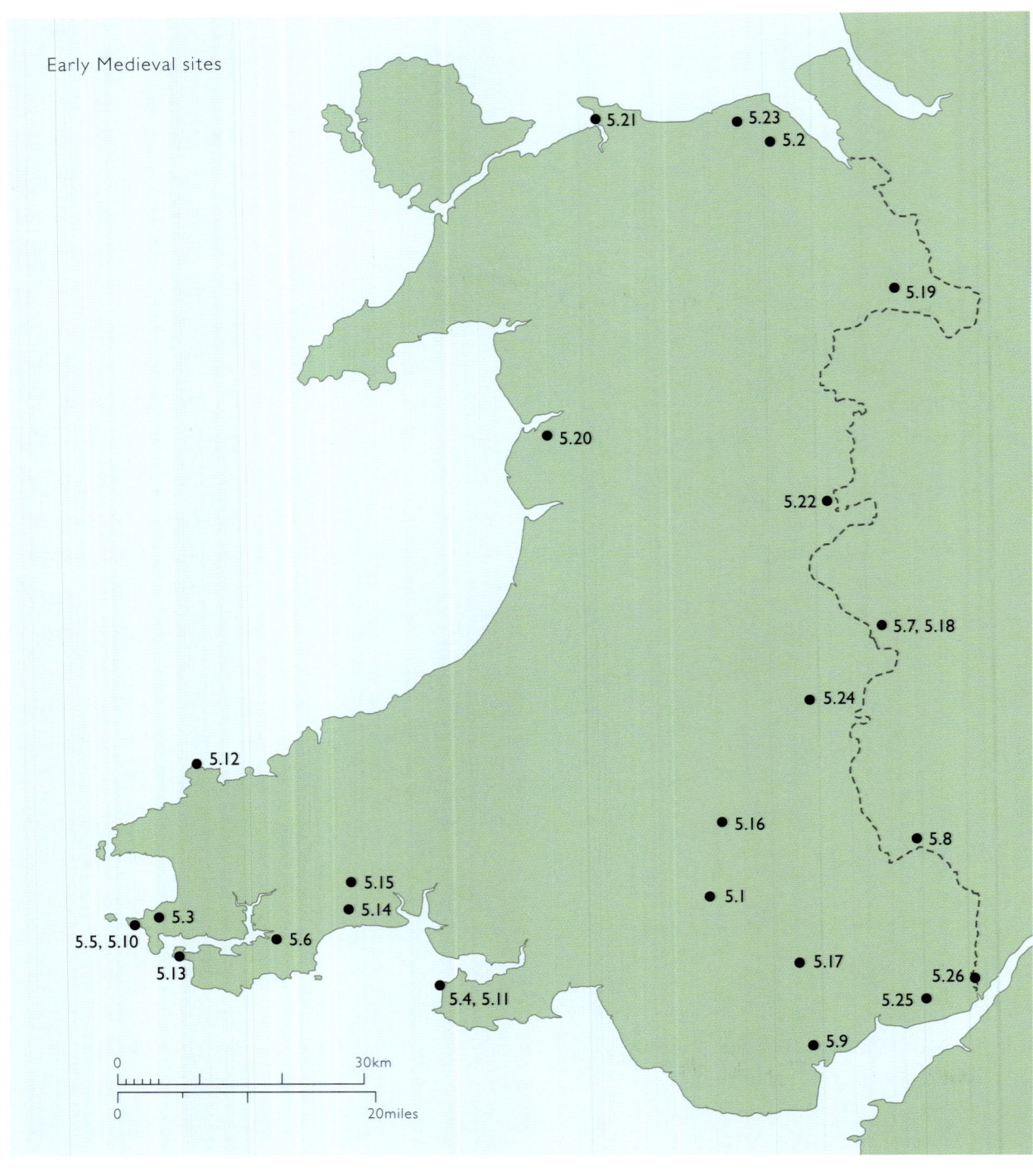

Early Medieval sites

5.21

5.23

5.2

5.19

5.20

5.22

5.7, 5.18

5.24

5.12

5.16

5.8

5.15

5.1

5.3

5.14

5.5, 5.10

5.6

5.17

5.26

5.13

5.25

5.4, 5.11

5.9

0   30km

0   20miles

5.

With the loss of support from the emperor, the Romanised towns and cities of Britain had to form their own government and establish a 'home guard' to deal with the increasing raids of pagan Saxons, Angles and Jutes from Europe. This is the time popularly known as the 'Dark Ages', although modern academics seem to prefer the less ominous sounding 'Early Medieval' period. However, from the perspective of this book, the time after the Romans left is indeed a dimly-lit hiatus, for there is little to catch the aerial photographer's eye until the Norman conquerors arrived and began to make their own mark upon the landscape.

For some Romano-British communities, a semblance of a civilised way of life continued for some years to come (and the most enduring legacy was the retention of Latin by those who could read and write); but over the next two centuries, the European migrants (collectively known as Anglo-Saxons) colonised south-east England and spread further west and north. The native Britons were pushed back into the furthest reaches of Cornwall, Wales and Scotland. In time, these isolated branches of the once widespread Celtic race would be identifying themselves as the *Cymry* ('fellow countrymen') and shared a common language and culture. The Anglo-Saxons, however, considered the natives whose lands they were busy colonising, to be 'foreigners' (*Wælisc*, or Welsh). To add to the cultural melting pot, an influx of migrants from southern Ireland settled in coastal districts of north and west Wales, their former presence attested to by the survival of memorial stones with distinctive notched Ogham script.

The collapse of centralised power enabled those with enough armed support and ambition to step into the void and establish their own hegemony. Out of the old Romano-British territories in Wales, a patchwork of small kingdoms gradually evolved, ruled by a warrior aristocracy. By AD 700 the principal realms were Gwynedd in the north, Powys in the midlands and Morgannwg (Glamorgan) in the south, along with the smaller kingdoms of Brycheiniog (Brecon), Gwent and Dyfed. Around AD 950 the latter was merged with two other territories to form the greater realm of Deheubarth. The boundaries of these lands fluctuated widely as rival rulers fought for supremacy and attempted to enlarge their dominions at the expense of others.

It was a time of almost incessant warfare, not just between the Welsh themselves, but also against the Anglo-Saxon rulers of Mercia (the great kingdom that abutted Powys to the east). Yet it was out of such turmoil that the country and society we now recognise as Wales and the Welsh was born.

For most of the inhabitants, life was a harsh and impoverished existence, being tied to the land on which they tilled and toiled. They lived in scattered farmsteads and small hamlets instead of the bustling urban centres of Roman times, and it was a settlement pattern that was to endure for many more centuries. Christianity had been adopted as the official religion of the empire in late-Roman times, and the Welsh continued to uphold their faith in the face of pagan Anglo-Saxon expansion. Efforts to convert the Saxons did not take place until St Augustine's mission to Kent in AD 597, but by that time monasticism was flourishing in the Celtic realms.

The fifth and sixth centuries are popularly known as the 'Age of Saints'. The Word of God was spread throughout the land by hermits and holy men, such as St Illtud (c.480–540), who founded an important monastery at Llantwit Major in the Vale of Glamorgan. This is reputed to have been the first centre of religious learning in Britain and drew students from as far afield as Cornwall, Ireland and Brittany. Among them was the historian Gildas and our future patron saint, David (Dewi Sant c.500–89). Other notable saints of the period included Beuno, Dyfrig, Padarn and Teilo. Their names are enshrined in medieval hagiographies, as well as commemorated by the dedication of churches that they, or their followers, established throughout the countryside.

The most tangible relic of these times are the numerous inscribed memorial stones that survive

Fig. 5.1 Maen Madoc inscribed stone

in various churches and museums. The earliest ones, believed to date from between AD 450 and 650, carry the name of the deceased and a simple Latin tag, as can be seen on Maen Madoc, beside the old Roman road at Ystradfellte (Fig. 5.1). Along the side of the pillar is a partial inscription reading *DERVAC- FILIUS IVSTI- (H)IC IACIT* ('Dervacus, son of Justus, he lies here'). These memorials were superseded by much plainer marker stones carved with a simple outline cross, but from the 800s the inscriptions reappear (one in Tywyn Church is unique in being written in early Welsh). From the 900s onwards craftsmen became ever more adept and inventive, carving complex patterns

LEFT: **Fig. 5.2** Maen Achwyfan decorated cross; RIGHT: **Fig. 5.3** St Brides Church and 'Celtic' crosses

and sinuous plaitwork designs onto monolithic slabs of stone, such as Maen Achwyfan near Whitford (Fig. 5.2), and the even larger crosses at Carew and Nevern in Pembrokeshire.

While the presence of these memorials points to the early-medieval origin of many Welsh churches, it must be remembered that the buildings themselves are almost always of a much later date, even though they may reflect a continuity of use throughout the centuries. St Bride's Church near Dale in south-west Pembrokeshire is a typical example (Fig. 5.3). The existing church is medieval, and the 'Celtic' crosses are Victorian, but slab-lined graves and an inscribed stone have been found here, proving that St Bride's was a genuine burial ground in the Early Medieval period.

The presence of circular (or near-circular) graveyards is another likely indicator of antiquity,

the walls marking the curvilinear boundaries of the early 'Llan' enclosure, as can be seen at Eglwys Gymyn (Fig. 5.14) and Merthyr Cynog (Fig. 5.16). Some of these enclosures are likely to be reused Iron Age hillforts. In the nineteenth century, stone-lined graves were found within the ramparts of Caerau Gaer, Moylgrove (Fig. 1.1), and an adjacent field was known as Yr Hen Fynachlog ('the old monastery'), suggesting it might have been the forerunner of nearby St Dogmael's Abbey. A small hillfort at Bayvil not far away was partially excavated in 1979 and found to be packed with burials orientated east-west in the Christian tradition.

Other excavations have revealed traces of small and simple structures predating the grander stone churches that replaced them. A good example is the small tidal islet of Burry Holms at the western end of Gower; the ruins of several buildings remain

Fig. 5.4 A reconstruction drawing showing how the pre-Norman church at Burry Holms may have looked

Fig. 5.5 Aerial view over Gateholm Island;

on the sheltered east side, but there is also a Bronze Age cairn here, an Iron Age promontory fort and evidence of Stone Age occupation stretching back around 9,000 years. In medieval times the islet was revered as the hermitage of St Cenydd, who lived in the sixth century and reputedly founded the nearby church of Llangennith. In 1965–8 archaeologists uncovered a graveyard enclosure with a small timber building beneath the ruins of the Norman period chapel (Fig. 5.4). The building was marked only by post-holes and measured just 3.3m by 5.2m, and was used as a shrine or a simple chapel. More post-holes outside the enclosure marked the site of a hut, presumably the humble dwelling of the resident priest. On Puffin Island (Anglesey) more substantial remains were excavated in 1900, consisting of rectangular stone huts or cells within a walled enclosure, but the site has recently become obscured by dense undergrowth. Other island sanctuaries of probable Early Medieval origin include Caldey (Tenby), Bardsey and St Tudwal's (both in Llŷn).

The largest and most mysterious of these offshore refuges is Gateholm near Marloes in south-west Pembrokeshire (Fig. 5.5). This can now only be reached by a difficult scramble at low tide, but may once have been a peninsula linked to the mainland. The flat summit of the island is speckled with the foundations of 100–150 hut sites, some round, but most sub-rectangular, and many linked together to form long terraces with attached courtyards and gardens. The walls of the buildings were constructed from a mix of turf with stone footings, while the roofs were presumably of thatch or turf. Limited excavations have taken place here over the years (in 1910, 1920 and most recently in 2013 by *Time Team*), but a convincing date has yet to be agreed upon. Finds have included Neolithic flints, Romano-British pottery, a sixth-century bronze pin and medieval pottery. Clearly the island has witnessed a long period of intermittent occupation, and a tantalising suggestion is that Gateholm was the site of an early monastic settlement, perhaps with a population in excess of 200. However, it has also been conjectured that the island was a secular, rather than an ecclesiastical site, rather like the better-known complex at Tintagel in Cornwall. If so, it would make a welcome addition to the skimpy list of Early Medieval secular sites in Wales.

From limited excavations and a scattering of archaeological finds, a picture emerges of a rural population eking out a meagre living in small huts and cave shelters, while some of the aristocracy chose to reoccupy Iron Age forts, either for status or defence. Contemporary documents make references to the *llys* (court) of a regional ruler, a complex of buildings featuring a great hall where

Fig. 5.6 Aerial view looking westwards over Carew

the monarch and his retinue would reside while on progress through the territory. But actual remains of such establishments are much harder to come by. Excavations have revealed the existence of a multivallate promontory fort beneath the later ruins of Carew Castle, which seems to have been reused as a *llys* by the ruling family of Deheubarth in the seventh century. The long-lost ditches of the fort can be seen as a series of dark bands crossing the field in front of the castle gate (Fig. 5.6). It may be no coincidence that the famous Celtic cross nearby carries an inscription to the memory of King Maredudd ap Edwin, who died in battle in 1035.

Other primitive hillfort-type citadels have been recognised at Dinas Powis (Glamorgan), Deganwy (Fig. 5.21) and Dinas Emrys (both in Gwynedd). The latter two have produced finds dating from the fifth to the thirteenth centuries, revealing that such inhospitable outcrops were favoured as refuges by the warlords of Early Medieval Wales. Uncomfortable and inconvenient they may have been, but a residence on such windswept heights not only gave good protection against attack, but blatantly displayed the power and authority of whoever lived there. The subsequent reuse of both locations as medieval castles shows a continuity of use, as Norman lords or Welsh princes sought to associate themselves with semi-legendary figures from the mythic past.

The most substantial monument built during this period is the great earthwork known as Offa's Dyke. At about 82 miles in length, this is reckoned to be the longest artificial construction in Britain (its nearest rival is the 73-mile-long Hadrian's Wall). The dyke runs intermittently from the Severn in the south to the Dee in the north, and consists of an earthen rampart fronted by a deep

Fig. 5.7 A well-preserved stretch of Offa's Dyke along Llanfair Hill near Knighton

ditch on its western (Welsh) side. Originally the bank may have stood over 2m high and was topped with a hedge or palisade. According to tradition it was built by Offa, king of Mercia, who reigned from AD 759 to 798. The only near-contemporary evidence we have for this is a statement made about a century later by a Welsh cleric named Asser, who wrote that Offa had ordered the building of 'a great dyke between Wales and Mercia from sea to sea'. In fact, the dyke was never quite as long as Asser implied. There are large gaps – particularly in Herefordshire – which suggest it was never even started there, or was perhaps served by natural obstacles such as the River Wye. In the north-east of the country the dyke fades out just north of Wrexham, where it is overlapped by a 28-mile

stretch of another linear earthwork, known as Wat's Dyke, stretching from Chirk to the Dee estuary.

For much of its length Offa's Dyke still acts as the border between Wales and England, but the condition of the earthwork varies considerably, and the most visually impressive sections are now in England (Figs 5.7 & 5.18). Was it meant to be a fortification, an obstacle to Welsh raiders plundering Anglo-Saxon lands or an agreed frontier line demarcating the limits of the independent kingdoms of Wales? Recent re-evaluations and evidence from radiocarbon dating suggest that although the dykes are of Early Medieval origin, they have widely differing phases of construction, and perhaps represent a long-term building project carried out by a succession of rulers, rather than one mammoth undertaking by a single figure.

Whatever the reason, the frontier did not hold back settlers from either side. The English colonised the lands west of the Dee, while the native warlords plundered and seized territory from their neighbours whenever the opportunity arose. To add to the turmoil, during the 800s Scandinavian Vikings increasingly carried out raids on vulnerable Welsh and English settlements, particularly those closest to the coast, where they could escape back to their longships with as much by way of goods and slaves as they could carry. Monasteries made for rich plunder, and the threat of God's vengeance held few fears for the pagan freebooters. Attempts were made at more permanent settlement, but apart from some archaeological finds and a scattering of Scandinavian place-names, it seems that the Vikings did not gain a lasting foothold in Wales, as they did in Ireland, the Isle of Man and north-east England. Fierce resistance from the Welsh leaders, particularly Rhodri Mawr (d.878) and his grandson Hywel Dda (d.950) saw to that.

The unquenchable desire for power and independence amongst the Welsh rulers resulted in an almost constant state of warfare, and contemporary chronicles paint a very depressing and bloodthirsty picture of the time. Greatest of these warlords was Gruffudd ap Llywelyn, who in 1039 began a campaign of warfare and regnal massacres to bring Wales under his sway. For a few years his goal was achieved, and Gruffudd garnered such strength and prestige that he was able to launch devastating raids into England, reducing the cathedral city of Hereford to a smouldering wreck, and forcing the Anglo-Saxon King Edward the Confessor to accept a humiliating truce. But

through the actions of untrustworthy allies and fierce opposition from the ambitious Harold Godwinson, earl of Wessex, Gruffudd was betrayed and murdered in 1063.

Some years prior to that date, King Edward had attempted to find a military solution to the persistent menace of the Welsh, and employed mercenary knights from Normandy to protect the vulnerable border. Ultimately, his plan backfired, for the Normans made themselves so objectionable to the Anglo-Saxon earls that they were forced out; though not before they had established a number of defended bases that featured a new type of fortification, called a 'castle' (after the Latin term *castrum*).

While it is usually assumed that castles only appeared in Britain in the wake of the Norman invasion of 1066, they were in fact here earlier than that iconic date (even though their first appearance

Fig. 5.8 Remains of the early castle of Ewyas Harold

was not an unqualified success). What may be the very first castle built in Britain stands on a hill above the village of Ewyas Harold, just over the border from Wales. This has been tentatively identified as the castle of Osbern Pentecost, mentioned in an entry for the year 1052 in the *Anglo-Saxon Chronicle*. It is now a rather uninspiring and densely overgrown mound (Fig. 5.8), but it shows the salient features of these new fortifications that were soon to pose a threat to native supremacy in Wales. The high, steep-sided mound, called a **motte**, would have been topped with a wooden tower that acted as the stronghold and last refuge of the garrison in the event of an attack. At its base lay a semi-circular embanked courtyard, the **bailey**, wherein stood various buildings including workshops, stores, stables, barracks and a residential hall for the castle's owner. The motte-and-bailey design proliferated throughout Wales in the coming years (Figs 5.9, 5.23 & 5.25).

Unlike the large-scale communal defensive works of previous ages, castles were intended to function as private fortified residences and military bases for the new ruling class. The majority were built by the invaders to consolidate their hold on conquered territories, but the design was gradually adopted by the Welsh themselves, to stabilise their own power in the face of both Norman and native aggression. Another type of fortification built in these early campaigns is termed a **ringwork**, and consists of an oval or circular embanked enclosure, rather like a small Iron Age hillfort.

When King Edward died in January 1066, Earl Harold was chosen to succeed, much to the fury of Duke William of Normandy, who optimistically believed that the throne should have been his. He won the argument by force of arms. Harold was killed along with the cream of the English nobility on the battlefield of Hastings nine months later. Within a few years Anglo-Saxon England had effectively ceased to be, and the lands and titles of the old regime had been redistributed among the new Norman aristocracy. Yet in Wales the native kings seemed oblivious to the danger posed by the new arrivals, and carried on with their petty feuds. They even employed Norman mercenaries to help with their power struggles.

King William, meanwhile, ordered the building of royal castles at Chester, Shrewsbury and Hereford, and established a frontier zone between Wales and England that in time became known as 'the March'. By 1070, trusted Norman warlords had been placed in positions of authority along the border and given free rein to seize Welsh land, which would then be distributed among their own followers in return for military support. Thus, a network of fortified bases quickly spread throughout the region, making the Welsh Marches one of the most heavily castellated areas of Britain. At first the castles were short-lived forts of timber construction (which frequently suffered from the fiery retribution of the Welsh) but in time, the more important and strategic bases were to be expensively rebuilt in durable masonry.

A temporary halt to the Norman advance occurred in 1081 when King William went on pilgrimage to St Davids Cathedral, and on the way reached an accord with Rhys ap Tewdwr, who had just survived a bloody civil war between the Welsh leaders. For a hefty sum of money Rhys was left in control of Deheubarth. Despite what the chroniclers claimed, the king's expedition was far more likely to be a show of power rather than a pious peregrination, and in order to signal his

Fig. 5.9 At the centre of Cardiff Castle is this massive motte, crowned with a later shell keep

authority a massive castle was built within the remains of the Roman fort at Cardiff (Fig. 5.9). This agreement bought a decade or so of relative peace, but their insatiable greed for Welsh land did not hold the Normans at bay for long. While defending his borders against further incursions in 1093, Rhys was killed in battle, and the floodgates were opened for a full-scale takeover. But if the Marcher lords thought that well-armed knights and rapidly-built castles would be enough to crush the Welsh, then they were greatly mistaken. The dogged persistence and savage strength of the native fighters meant that the conquest of Wales was to be dragged out over the next two centuries.

Figs 5.10a & 5.10b Gateholm Island, Marloes
(SM 769 073). Now accessible only at low tide, Gateholm was probably originally reached along an isthmus before coastal erosion broke the connection with the mainland. The plateau bears the scars of well over 100 sub-rectangular huts, most linked together to form long terraces, suggesting that a large population lived on this exposed headland. The view (above) looks across the island to the south-east, the low winter sun highlighting many of the more obvious huts. The drawing (left) shows how just part of the site may have looked originally. The wide range of finds point to a long period of intermittent occupation from Roman times to the Middle Ages.

Figs 5.11a & 5.11b Burry Holms, Gower (SS 401 926). Like Gateholm, this small island can only be reached at low tide, but in earlier times it was far more accessible, and evidence of around 9,000 years of intermittent human occupation can be found here. In medieval times an ecclesiastical settlement was established on the more sheltered east side. The ruins of the twelfth-century chapel can be seen in the foreground (right), with the outlines of a later residential hall beyond. Excavators found the remains of a pre-Norman burial site beneath the chapel, which may date back to the sixth century and the time of its founder, St Cenydd. The enclosure contained several graves and a small timber structure, perhaps a shrine or early chapel (see reconstruction Fig. 5.4).

Figs 5.12a & 5.12b Strumble Head, Fishguard (SM 893 413). The dramatically situated Strumble Head lighthouse was built on Ynys Meicel in 1908 to guide ships past the rugged Pencaer Peninsula. The existing aluminium bridge replaced an earlier iron one in 1963, and the lighthouse was fully automated in 1980. On the south side of the island the remains of several rectangular buildings terraced into the slope can be seen. Given the predilection of early saints and hermits for inaccessible islands, coupled with the place-name (St Michael's Isle), this could be the remains of an early-medieval ecclesiastical settlement, although this has yet to be proven by archaeological investigaton.

Figs 5.13a & 5.13b Sheep Island, Angle (SM 846 017). Also known as Castles Bay Camp, this Iron Age fort can easily be seen from the coast path near the entrance to the Milford Haven waterway. The middle section of the headland (above, looking south), is pockmarked with rock-cut hollows that mark the remains of numerous sub-rectangular buildings. Masonry foundations of a gate-tower, rock-cut steps and an earthen rampart can still be seen on the side facing the isthmus (which is crumbling away at an alarming rate). Back in 1603 the antiquarian George Owen noted the ruined tower, and considered the site was a fortified refuge for Norman settlers, but the similarity of these features to Gateholm suggest that this might potentially be another Early Medieval coastal settlement.

Fig. 5.14 Eglwys Gymyn, Pendine (SN 230 107). A classic example of a circular churchyard enclosure, Eglwys Gymyn lies on a hilltop at the intersection of several tracks, and its elevated location suggests it may have been a reused Iron Age or Romano-British settlement site. Slight earthworks in the adjacent fields mark the remains of a deserted medieval village. This view shows the site from the north. The church contains a fifth- or sixth-century stone inscribed in both Latin and Irish Ogham.

Fig. 5.15 Llangan near Whitland (SN 177 187). This is a view from the south of the circular churchyard. Cropmark photos have revealed that the churchyard lies just inside a much larger Prehistoric enclosure. Unfortunately, the Victorian church is now derelict and in decay, and an inscribed boulder that stood nearby has disappeared (even though it is still marked on OS maps as 'St Canna's Chair'). These Carmarthenshire churches are clearly of Early Christian origin, even though the actual fabric of the buildings is much later in date.

Fig. 5.16 Merthyr Cynog, near Brecon (SN 984 375). Like Eglwys Gymyn, this is another good example of a circular churchyard located on a hilltop and at the junction of several old trackways. The graveyard is embanked and rises above the isolated village, suggesting t occupies the site of an older hillfort. Although no inscribed stones survive here, it is dedicated to the fifth-century St Cynog (one of the sons of King Brychan Brycheiniog) who was killed by pagan Saxons and buried here, hence the place-name ('Merthyr' means martyr). Pilgrims came here in medieval times to venerate a gold torque (a neck ornament) that was said to belong to the saint.

Figs 5.17a & 5.17b Capel Gwladys, Gelligaer (SO 125 993).
High on the moors separating the former mining valleys of the
South Wales coalfield, stands this little-known site, dedicated
to St Gwladys, one of the daughters of King Brychan. The
Celtic Cross and stone foundations are modern recreations,
but a slab incised with a ring-cross was discovered here in
1906 and removed to the parish church for safe keeping. At
the time traces of a nave, chancel and west tower were noted,
which probably represent a medieval replacement for the Early
Medieval chapel. The aerial view shows clearly the outlines of a
sub-rectangular enclosure surrounding the chapel, but there are
subtler earthworks suggesting that this was just a small part of a
complex upland site. The corduroy pattern of old ploughmarks
can be seen on the right, indicating that crops were once grown
on this bleak and unwelcoming landscape.

ABOVE: **Fig. 5.18 Offa's Dyke, Knighton** (SO 253 784). The earthwork boundary marker traditionally associated with King Offa of Mercia (d.798) runs for about 82 miles and still forms the border between England and Wales in places. Its course is also marked by the Offa's Dyke Long Distance Path. This view looks north-west along one of the best-preserved stretches of the dyke (now in England) along Llanfair Hill at Knighton Near Wrexham, the dyke is overlapped by another earthwork known as Wat's Dyke.

LEFT: **Wat's Dyke Fig. 5.19** (SJ 321 457) completes the missing section as far as the Dee estuary. In this view looking south towards Ruabon, the dyke is marked by a straight line of trees in the foreground, changing course after it is crossed by the B5426 road.

Fig. 5.20 Llys Bradwen, Dolgellau (SH 650 138). In this panoramic view northwards over the Mawddach estuary, a rectangular walled enclosure in the foreground is sharply defined by the early morning sun. The site consists of a levelled terrace reinforced with massive boulders, forming a walled courtyard that presumably once contained stone or timber buildings. There is a small annexe to the right. Tradition identifies this as a *llys* (court) of Bradwen ap Idnerth, founder of a local dynasty in the early twelfth century. Whether it does represent one of the few tangible relics of a native Welsh *llys* is open to question, for Roman pottery has also been found here, suggesting it may have had a much earlier origin. The site is evidently ancient, and the plough marks are clearly later as they respect the pre-existence of the enclosure and swerve to avoid it. Sharp-eyed readers may just pick out an ancient-looking clapper bridge crossing the stream, while out of shot to the left is a ruined building thought to be the site of a medieval chapel.

Fig. 5.21 Deganwy Castle, Llandudno (SH 783 796). The rock of Deganwy on the edge of the Conwy estuary has been intermittently occupied since late-Roman times. While the most obvious remains are now the shattered walls of a medieval castle, excavations here in the 1960s revealed traces of a drystone rampart that defended the main summit in far earlier days. Documentary evidence (and legend) points to the site as the stronghold of King Maelgwn Gwynedd (d.c.547), and fragments of imported Mediterranean pottery of roughly that period have been found here. The Early Medieval *Arx Decantorum* ('fortress of the Decanti') was burnt by lightning in 812, and attacked and destroyed by Anglo-Saxon raiders in 822. The defences were rebuilt on many occasions, but when King Edward I defeated the Welsh Princes in the 1280s, ancient Deganwy was abandoned in favour of a new castle across the river at Conwy (seen in the background). This view shows the larger of the hill's twin peaks from the north; some of the ruined medieval walls are visible in the foreground, while the big central pit is either a quarry or a cistern.

Fig. 5.22 Hen Domen, Montgomery
(SO 214 980). Tree-cover regrettably obscures so much of this key site, which is not only one of the earliest castles in the Welsh Marches, but also the setting for the most detailed and lengthy series of excavations (1960–92) ever carried out on a wooden castle. It had been built by the earl of Shrewsbury around 1071, who named it after his home town of Montgomery in Normandy. The various digs revealed fascinating details about the timber structures and buildings that crammed the interior of the castle. In this view, looking south, the motte can just be glimpsed to the right, with the oval bailey extending to the left. The whole of this site was surrounded by an outer rampart, with ditches that still hold water to this day.

Fig. 5.23 Twthill, Rhuddlan (SJ 026 777). Twthill is another motte-and-bailey set up in the early years of the Norman advance, and its founder chose to adopt the place-name for his own. Robert of Rhuddlan was a kinsman of the earl of Chester and was allowed to plunder westwards to his heart's content. By the time of Domesday Book (1086) he was said to be in control of the whole of North Wales. In this view the motte is prominent in the foreground, while beyond, the river winds northwards past the ruins of the later castle to the sea at Rhyl.

Fig. 5.24 Castell Crugerydd, New Radnor (SO 157 593). Prominently situated beside the A44 as it crosses a mountain pass, this classic example of the motte-and-bailey design is refreshingly free from the undergrowth that so often camouflages such earthworks. The origin of the castle is obscure, but it may have been built as an outpost to guard the route to the larger Norman base at New Radnor, or it may have been built by the Welsh themselves to protect their borders. It was certainly in native control when the cleric and chronicler Gerald of Wales was a guest of the local prince at 'Cruker Castle' in 1188.

Fig. 5.25 Caerwent 'motte' (ST 471 904). This modest, unrecorded mound, historically identified as a motte, is prominently situated at the south-east corner of the Roman walled town. It shows how the Normans were capable of adapting earlier fortifications to their own ends, whether for convenience or for strategic purposes. The mound would have made an ideal look-out for soldiers garrisoned within the walls, but as there is no sign of a bailey, or any attempt to make a more lasting castle here, it may have been just a short-term base as they pushed westwards. An intriguing suggestion is that the little castle guarded the workers pillaging Roman masonry for use elsewhere, particularly at nearby Chepstow Castle (see below).

Fig. 5.26 Chepstow Castle, Chepstow (ST 534 942). This is one of the very few castles in Britain built in stone from the start. Here, on an unassailable rocky eminence high above the tidal reaches of the Wye, a grand hall block was constructed at the end of the eleventh century, utilising reused Roman masonry. It stands in the centre of this view, looking westwards across the walls and towers added at a later date. The upper floor is also a later modification, and when first built it consisted of a low dark basement with a large first-floor chamber, used perhaps as an audience chamber on ceremonial occasions, as well as providing lordly accommodation. However, there is much controversy as to when it was built. Domesday Book (1086) states that Chepstow was built by William FitzOsbern, one of William the Conqueror's most loyal followers, who had been made earl of Hereford and undertook the conquest of the Welsh kingdom of Gwent. Some historians doubt whether there was enough time or inclination for FitzOsbern to raise such an expensive structure on the volatile frontier before he was killed in battle in 1071; therefore, it may have been built by royal masons after the earldom had passed into the king's hands in 1075. Whoever was responsible for its construction, the castle was a bold statement of Norman power and ambition.

OPPOSITE: A near vertical view of the walls and towers of White Castle, Monmouthshire

Medieval sites

6.79 6.88
6.51
6.78
6.77 6.50 6.39
6.5 6.14
6.40
6.83
6.41
6.48
6.67
6.68
6.93 6.42

6.31
6.47
6.4, 6.45
6.46

6.70

6.76

6.85
6.53
6.69
6.34

6.3

6.61
6.64
6.66
6.6, 6.7, 6.86

6.63, 6.65
6.26
6.28
6.62

6.29
6.27
6.16

6.58

6.57
6.74

6.87

6.56
6.44
6.94
6.71
6.55

6.98
6.84 6.33 6.12
6.37 6.36
6.38
6.17, 6.24
6.13, 6.59
6.32
6.22 6.81
6.23, 6.72

6.96
6.95
6.82

6.11

6.15

6.35
6.30 6.8,
6.52 6.97
6.21,
6.3
6.92
6.25

6.43

6.19, 6.20
6.80
6.73
6.1, 6.18, 6.89 6.54 6.60
6.10, 6.90, 6.91

0   30km

0   20miles

TOWERS AND BATTLEMENTS

AFTER 1093 THE Norman invaders intensified their campaigns in Wales, seizing native lands and securing their gains by building numerous castles. Inroads were made into the south and west of the country, leading to the more or less permanent colonisation of parts of Pembrokeshire and Glamorgan. A string of military bases and fortified settlements had been established in the Marches, including New Radnor (Fig. 6.29), Hay-on-Wye (Fig. 6.57) and Brecon (Fig. 6.56), which were used as springboards for further advance. Beyond these strongholds, the land was largely under Welsh control, and for the next 200 years the country was racked by the ebb and flow of war, as territories were won and lost, and periods of uneasy peace were shattered by outbreaks of savage fighting. The English kings and the Marcher lords sought to enforce their control over the native princes, but the results were always temporary, as a succession of figures – such as Owain Gwynedd, Lord Rhys and Llywelyn the Great – fought back.

The wooden castles that had proliferated during the initial invasions were cheap and quick to build, but they could not withstand concerted attacks, and the chronicles of the time record their frequent destruction. By today they have invariably been reduced to overgrown earthworks, and the elaborate timber structures that once crowned them have long disappeared, only to be revealed as a pattern of post-holes and buried foundations during archaeological excavations. To replace timber with more durable stonework was therefore a necessary step to ensure the longevity of a castle, but masonry construction was a costly and time-consuming affair that required the use of skilled craftsmen. Therefore, it was only carried out on very important and strategic sites and the scale of the final product depended very much on the available resources and wealth of the builder. The grandest buildings of all were the work of the king and his more important barons.

Often it was the principal tower (commonly known as the keep) that was the first part to be rebuilt in stone. This provided secure accommodation and a refuge from attack, as well as serving as a highly-visible symbol of Norman authority. The timber palisades and outworks would be replaced by high stone curtain walls, perhaps with projecting turrets to enable the defending garrison to overlook the perimeter and target any

Fig. 6.1 Cutaway reconstruction of the keep at Ogmore

attacker. Outer ditches and water-filled moats served to keep the enemy and their siege machines at bay.

Twelfth-century masonry castles usually had fairly simple layouts. Bridgend in Glamorgan is one of the most intact Norman castles in Wales, little changed in subsequent years and consisting of a polygonal walled enclosure with two square flanking towers (Fig. 6.20). A similar plan was adopted at nearby Coity (Fig. 6.19) and, despite many later alterations, the outline of the original timber ringwork is still very apparent from the air. Not too far away at Ogmore (Figs 6.1 & 6.18), another twelfth-century ringwork castle was strengthened with the addition of a rather grand little keep. The inner wall has since fallen away, providing modern visitors with a cross-section view through the building. The ground floor was a dark and basic storeroom, while on the first floor there was a residential apartment, apparently divided in two by a timber screen; one half perhaps served as an assembly hall, while the other half was a more comfortable living room heated by an enormous fireplace.

By the start of the thirteenth century, new architectural fashions began to appear, and more ambitious designs were tried out. Towers were increasingly built to a rounded or D-shaped plan, and boldly jutted out from the curtain walls so that archers and crossbow-men safely positioned inside could target the approach of any attacker. Gateways were heavily defended with drawbridges and portcullises, and the entry passage was usually set between a pair of flanking towers to give forward protection from attack. The twin-towered gatehouse at Chepstow (Fig. 6.2) is one of the earliest of this design built in Wales. The wooden doors have been dated to no later than 1189, although there is some controversy about the age of the adjoining towers (they may be slightly later additions). Chepstow was one of the many castles held by the wealthy

Fig. 6.2 The twin-towered gatehouse at Chepstow

and powerful William Marshal, earl of Pembroke who built an enormous round keep at the seat of his earldom (Fig. 6.23). Other Marcher lords soon followed suit.

The threat posed by these new stone castles was not lost on the Welsh princes, who responded in kind with their own fortifications. With smaller revenues and without the benefit of skilled engineers, their castles were generally much more modest constructions and usually lacked the finesse of the Anglo-Norman designers. Nevertheless, they were well-suited to the native way of fighting and were built to make the most of the natural rugged terrain (Figs 6.38–6.42).

It was to take a warrior king of exceptional ability and ruthless determination to end the age of the independent princes. Towards the close of the thirteenth century, King Edward I of England embarked on two military campaigns to tame the ambitions of the powerful ruler of

Fig. 6.3 Reconstruction of Castell Bryn Amlwg on the Welsh border, after the original earthwork defences had been upgraded with masonry

Gwynedd, Llywelyn ap Gruffudd, who had achieved overlordship over the other Welsh leaders. Llywelyn was killed in battle in 1282, enabling the king to impose his iron rule upon the country and embark on the most expensive and ambitious scheme of castle-building ever undertaken by the English Crown. Using the most advanced military techniques and building skills that money could buy, King Edward's great castles were designed to intimidate the native population and crush any attempt to remove the yoke of English domination. These vast edifices represent the peak of medieval castle-building in the country, and display a range of designs adapted to suit each locale. In the south the old motte-and-bailey of Builth was reconstructed as an imposing stone fortress – though the passer-by would be hard-pressed to appreciate this now (see Fig. 6.28). The coastal stronghold of Aberystwyth was a wholly new structure, built to a concentric layout (one line of defence within another), a plan that was similarly adopted at Harlech (Fig. 6.48) and Rhuddlan (Fig. 6.47). Conwy and Caernarfon were little more that walled courtyards bulging with massive flanking towers of varying shapes (Figs 6.49 & 6.50). Strangest of all was Flint (Figs 6.4 & 6.45), built to a superficially simple layout, but with a detached cylindrical keep of such peculiar design that it defies understanding to this day.

The majority of these castles were built in tandem with fortified towns reserved for English settlers and merchants. New laws and harsh penalties effectively reduced the Welsh to second-class citizens in their own country. Even in the face of such an overwhelming and costly scheme of suppression, unrest continued for several decades. After a widespread revolt in 1294–5 the king embarked on his last major undertaking in Wales, a brand-new castle at Beaumaris on Anglesey (Fig. 6.51). Beaumaris should have been one of the greatest architectural showpieces in Western Europe, but as the flames of rebellion flickered out and the belligerent Edward turned his attention to Scotland, the money dried up and the building was left incomplete. The massive towers are as stunted now as they were on the day the workmen downed tools.

The military need for castles waned as the fourteenth century progressed. Many of the royal fortresses were reported to be in a very poor state just a few decades after they had been built. Frontline castles, hurriedly raised in strategic or remote locations, now found themselves without a viable purpose and so were neglected or abandoned. Rich lords and absentee landowners preferred to spend their money on improving the domestic comforts on offer at their principal properties. The earl of Norfolk built a luxurious residence within the walls of Chepstow, the great hall at Caerphilly was revamped on a palatial scale, while at Tretower (Fig. 6.71) the owners decamped to a new and undefended house beside their antiquated fortress. In some cases the outwardly military aspect of the castle was face-lifted onto more modest residences to provide the occupiers with a veneer of defensibility.

The uprising of Owain Glyndŵr in 1400 came as a violent shock to the complacency of the English oppressors, and led to a decade of unrest and attrition throughout Wales and the Marches. The new Lancastrian ruler Henry IV ordered those who had castles capable of defence to ensure that they were up to scratch, and so a flurry of repairs and rebuilding took place. However, by and large castles now had less of a role to play in warfare, and the outcome of the revolt (as well as the episodic bouts of violence that fractured aristocratic society during the fifteenth century) would be decided on the battlefield rather than by long-drawn-out sieges.

The appearance of artillery weapons had also prompted changes to the design of castles. These changes were at first relatively minor and tentative, such as the gunports alongside the archaic arrow-slits at Raglan in Monmouthshire (Fig. 6.52), the last major castle to be built in Wales. Early guns were quite primitive weapons and could be as dangerous to the operators as much as to the intended targets, but advances in technology soon led to more efficient weapons. The high walls and tall towers that had for so long kept the warrior aristocracy safe, were no longer tenable. Purpose-built artillery forts made their appearance towards the close of the fifteenth century, and with the wide social changes brought about by the relatively stable

Fig. 6.4 Conjectural reconstruction of King Edward's castle at Flint, as it might have looked in 1301

government of the Tudor monarchy, there was little need for private armies and personal fortifications. The decline of the castle in Wales and southern England was rapid, and by the 1540s antiquarian accounts depict a countryside dotted with the crumbling remains of abandoned buildings, their stones pillaged for reuse elsewhere. Only a very few remained in occupation, their warlike façades tamed and their spartan interiors transformed to suit the comforts of the time. Montgomery (Fig. 6.34) and Raglan (Fig. 6.52) fell victim to the English Civil War of 1642–51 and were never restored, while Cardiff Castle, Powis Castle (Fig. 6.53) and St Donat's (Fig. 6.54) managed to survive and, having undergone bouts of refurbishment, remain occupied to this day.

CHURCH AND CLOISTER

The Anglo-Norman invaders were not only intent on securing their hold on Wales through military action, but through ecclesiastical means as well. Religion was an ingrained aspect of life, culture and politics in medieval Britain. Simple churches and monastic communities were dotted throughout the land. Priests and monks were usually the most educated members of society, and they alone could offer the promise of salvation to the illiterate and hard-working masses. As more Welsh territory was appropriated, churches that had been founded by, or had been named in memory of, ancient Celtic holy men, ended up being rededicated to saints more familiar to the conquerors (and usually with names that were easier to pronounce). New pro-Norman bishops were installed in native cathedrals and the overlordship of Canterbury was grudgingly acknowledged. The early churches were often simple structures, built from stone and wood, and

Fig. 6.5 Clynnog Fawr is one of the finest late-medieval churches in North Wales, rebuilt around 1500 to a cruciform plan with a western tower

containing a single room (the **nave**) where the faithful gathered to worship; but when sufficient funds became available, they were rebuilt on a larger scale, usually with a **chancel** at the east end containing the high altar, and perhaps a porch to cover the entrance. Many were graced with a tower, which was usually (but not invariably) positioned at the west end of the nave (Fig. 6.5).

The Norman invaders had little toleration for the home-grown Celtic monasticism and so these establishments too were re-founded along the lines of the more orthodox orders flourishing on the Continent. European communities followed the rules set down by the founding father of western monasticism, St Benedict (d.c.548). Benedictine monks took vows of obedience, chastity and poverty, and withdrew from society to spend their lives, from dawn to dusk, in a routine of communal prayer and manual labour. Other orders soon spread through Europe, such as the Cluniacs

LEFT: **Fig. 6.6** The western doorway of Strata Florida; RIGHT: **Fig. 6.7** A reconstruction of how Strata Florida might have appeared around 1500

and Carthusians, who also based their beliefs on variations of St Benedict's teachings. The monks distinguished themselves from other orders by the style and colour of the garments they wore.

One group that made a particular impact on the society and culture of Wales had been founded in eastern France in 1098. Known as the Cistercians (after their mother house at Cîteaux), these white-robed monks sought a much more austere and hard-working existence than the other orders, setting up their self-sufficient communes far from the distractions of urban life, where upland acres and marginal wastes could be turned into productive land. They arrived in England in 1128 and three years later established their

first community in Wales, at Tintern in the Wye Valley. Their hardy way of life crossed the cultural divide, finding favour with the belligerent Welsh princes who allowed the foundation of Cistercian monasteries within their territories. Of these, the most notable was Strata Florida, known in Welsh as Ystrad Fflur 'the Vale of Flowers' (Figs 6.6 & 6.7). Although it was originally a Norman foundation, it was re-established in 1184 by the Lord Rhys of Deheubarth and become a mausoleum for subsequent members of his dynasty. Around the same time, Rhys founded an abbey at Talley (Fig. 6.87) for the Premonstratensian order (the only such community in Wales), and also a Cistercian nunnery at Llanllyr, of which no trace survives today. This, however, was one of only four nunneries in the whole of Wales, a tiny number compared to the rest of medieval Britain, which suggests that the devout rigours of monastic life did not appeal as much to women as they did to men.

As the thirteenth century progressed, there was a further diversification with the arrival from the Continent of mendicant orders following the teachings of St Augustine (Augustinians), St Dominic (Dominicans) and St Francis of Assisi (Franciscans). They were known as friars, and aimed for a life of extreme poverty and simplicity. Having renounced material wealth, they relied entirely on charitable alms. Unlike monks cloistered away in their remote monasteries, friars actively travelled around and interacted with local communities, serving the poor and preaching the Gospel. They, too, were gifted with lands and property, and built numerous friaries in urban areas (there were nine in Wales, and the ruins of two can still be seen in Denbigh town and Bute Park, Cardiff). Their assets, incidentally, were held in trust, so that their vows of poverty would not be compromised.

Despite all the gifts and endowments received from their native benefactors, none of the Welsh monasteries ever grew to be as wealthy as those established by the Anglo-Normans, nor were their buildings as grand. There is clear evidence that ambitious schemes were changed or severely curtailed when the funding dried up. Abbey Cwmhir was intended to have an enormously long nave (at about 250 feet in length, it would have rivalled Canterbury Cathedral), but it appears that the full scheme was never carried through. Both Cymer and Talley abbeys had to be completed to truncated designs that failed to match the vision of their original founders.

In contrast the wealthier Norman establishments could rely on more generous patrons who might draw on revenues from outside war-torn Wales. Thus it was that in 1269 the munificence of the fifth earl of Norfolk enabled the Cistercian abbey at Tintern to be rebuilt on a magnificent scale, so that it is now among the grandest and most sublime of all monastic ruins in Britain (Fig. 6.8, overleaf).

The architecture of medieval monasteries tended to follow a broadly similar pattern. The most important building was the church itself. It was usually the first part to be built, and was as large and as splendid as the community could afford to make it. It was set out on a cross-shaped (cruciform) plan, comprising a chancel at the eastern end, then a pair of transepts at 90 degrees (often with a tower above the central crossing space), and finally the long arm of the nave (Fig. 6.9). In a few cases, however, the monastic church was an altogether more modest affair, hardly more ambitious that a local parish church, and comprising just a chancel and nave, perhaps with the additional flourish of a bell-tower. Outside the church, in the angle between the nave and one of the transepts, there would be a rectangular garden with an enclosed walkway, known as a cloister. Additional buildings were arranged around the cloister, including a dormitory, a dining hall (refectory) and a chapter house. The latter was basically a large room where the community would gather to discuss any pertinent issues, and listen to readings from the rules of their order. Other buildings within the monastic precinct might include a separate dwelling for the abbot, a kitchen, an infirmary, various workshops and storehouses, and accommodation for pilgrims and visiting dignitaries.

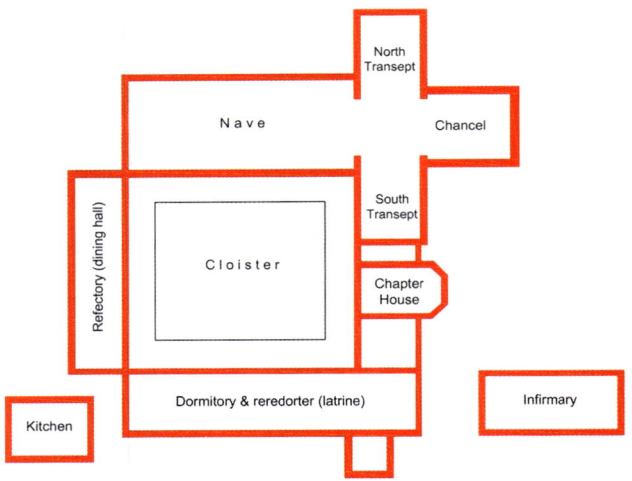

TOP: **Fig. 6.8** A view of the abbey church at Tintern
BOTTOM: **Fig. 6.9** A simplified plan of a typical monastic layout

Beyond the precinct walls lay the agricultural estates that had been granted to the monastery, and upon which it depended for revenues and produce. A monastic farm, or **grange**, would be established to manage the running of these estates. Each monastery usually had a number of granges, some located close by (the Cistercians at first ruled that a grange should be no more than a day's journey away, so that workers could return to the abbey for Sunday worship); but most were at a greater distance – indeed, wherever the gifted property lay. Dore Abbey in Herefordshire, for instance, had land in the Wye Valley near Builth Wells, while Tewkesbury Abbey in Gloucestershire had granges at Llandough and Llantwit Major in Glamorgan.

The granges were usually run either by the monks themselves, by hired labourers or by lay-brothers (illiterate, hard-working members of the monastic community who had not taken holy orders). In later medieval times there was a tendency for monasteries to lease out their estates to secular tenants in return for rent and produce, rather than working the lands direct. This process accelerated after the Reformation when all monastic property was seized by the Crown. Thereafter, some granges were abandoned while others continued to function, becoming all but indistinguishable from normal farmsteads, apart from a few archaeological traces or place-name evidence.

The buildings that constituted the grange varied considerably depending on the size and wealth of the estate. There were enormously large sheep farms in the uplands (Aberconwy Abbey held over 8,000 acres on the Denbigh Moors, while Margam and Neath in Glamorgan were recorded in possession of over 10,000 sheep in 1291). However, the actual grange buildings are likely to have been fairly unsophisticated structures, comprising just a few pens or shelters for the animals and a modest dwelling for the workers, contained within a fenced or hedged enclosure. Other granges were on an altogether different scale and featured the sort of buildings that might be found on any large country

Fig. 6.10 The ruined dovecote at Monknash grange

Fig. 6.11 A view of the fishtraps in Swansea Bay

estate, such as barns, granaries, dovecotes, stables and cowsheds. There would be residential quarters for the workers, perhaps a chapel for on-site worship, a mill for grinding locally-produced corn, and fish ponds to supply the monastery with food during Lent. The finest surviving granges in Wales are to be seen at Monknash (Figs 6.10 & 6.91) and Marcross (Fig. 6.90), both established by the monks of Neath Abbey to exploit their endowments in the fertile Vale of Glamorgan. Monknash is by far the most impressive when seen from the air, a vast 20-acre enclosure covered with a palimpsest of earthworks that marks the site of various buildings, garden plots and roadways. There is also a pepper pot-shaped dovecote and an enormous ruined barn, estimated to have been capable of storing 2,500 cubic metres of grain.

Another relic of medieval food production can be seen in certain places along the Welsh coastline. As the tide ebbs, the crumbling remains of stone walls are exposed to view. These stony scatters may be mistaken for natural banks of shingle by people walking along the beach, but from the air they show up as straight lines extending for hundreds of metres, incontrovertible proof that they are artificial constructions. However, these walls are not relics of mythical drowned kingdoms, as folklore might suggest, but the more mundane remains of **fishtraps** (*goradau* in Welsh). When first built they consisted of drystone walls reinforced with wattles and timber posts, and set in a right-angled or V-shaped arrangement (Fig. 6.11). The pointed end faced towards the lowest part of the beach, so that as the water level dropped, any fish caught within the tidal pool would be drawn towards the waiting nets at the apex of the trap. A prominent fishtrap can be seen extending out to sea near St Trillo's Chapel at Colwyn Bay, and is known as the Royal Fishing Weir. In the thirteenth century the fisheries here belonged to Aberconwy Abbey, but passed to the Crown in 1536. The trap was reportedly dismantled in 1550, but it was evidently restored and remained in use well into the nineteenth century (a record catch of 35,000 herrings made here in 1850). At low tide over two dozen traps can be seen along the broad sweep of Swansea Bay; some joined to form long W-shaped patterns, others overlapping – clear proof of extensive rebuilding and realignment as the tidal currents changed over the years.

Another important source of food for the medieval nobility was the rabbit. These non-indigenous animals may have been introduced into Britain by the Romans, but it was from Norman times onwards that they became prized as a source of meat and fur, and were farmed on an almost industrial scale. Warrens were considered a valuable asset by wealthy landowners (both secular and ecclesiastical) and were carefully guarded against poachers and predators. Rabbit farming has left its mark on the landscape too, in the form of elongated earthen mounds with side ditches, which were invariably built on sloping ground for drainage. These constructions have been termed **pillow mounds** – although, to be pedantic, they tend to be more cigar-shaped than pillow-shaped and (for no apparent reason) they were also built in round, oval and cruciform shapes as well (Fig. 6.94). Whatever the form adopted, all the mounds served the same purpose, to provide the animals with somewhere clean, dry and easy to dig into, where they would remain and breed like … well, rabbits. Pillow mounds can be found singly or in small groups, but are often clustered together in concentrations that denote the former existence of large upland warrens. While many of the mounds are likely to be medieval, others are of much more recent date, since rabbit farming continued into the nineteenth century. Thereafter the trade in meat and fur declined as the rabbit spread into the wild, and was seen as little more than a pest, fit only to be eaten by the poor.

By the start of the sixteenth century the founding fervour of monasticism had long since petered out. Many religious houses contained only a handful of inhabitants, their vast buildings sparsely used and much of their land leased out to secular tenants. There was clearly a need for some reform, but what actually occurred was ruthless suppression and state-sponsored vandalism on a scale unparalleled in British history. The Protestant reforms ushered in by king and Parliament signalled the end of the monasteries, along with shrines, Catholic festivals and popular places of pilgrimage. Almost 900 religious houses in Britain were closed between 1536 and 1540. Their buildings and assets were surrendered to the Crown and then sold off to wealthy landowners to fill the royal coffers.

The monastic buildings were quickly stripped of any valuable materials and in many cases demolished, so that only ruins and foundations remain to this day. The great nave of Abbey Cwmhir was ransacked, and the fine hammerbeam roof and dressed stone arcades were taken away and incorporated into the parish church at Llanidloes. Strata Marcella was considered to have been one of the largest monasteries in Wales, but is now little more than an inconspicuous jumble of earthworks in a field near Welshpool (Fig. 6.85). Some sites have disappeared altogether. No one really knows the exact location of Llanllyr nunnery, nor under which field in Monmouthshire the foundations

Fig. 6.12 The former priory church at St Clears

Fig. 6.13 This imposing town gate at Tenby is now known as 'The Five Arches'

of Grace Dieu Abbey might lie. In other cases the churches (or parts of them at least) were preserved so that they could be used for worship by the local parishioners. Of these fortunate few, Penmon (Fig. 6.88) and Ewenny (Fig. 6.89) still retain substantial portions of their monastic buildings, but Abergavenny, Beddgelert, Cardigan, Llangennith, Kidwelly and St Clears (Figs 6.12, 6.82 & 6.83), now look like 'normal' churches and display few signs of their monastic origins. Other structures associated with the monastery found uses as agricultural outbuildings, or were converted into domestic residences by their new secular owners.

HOUSE AND HOME

With a castle for military protection and a church for spiritual comfort, the English conquerors were able to impose a more structured approach to urban planning than was the norm in the Welsh countryside. Houses were grouped about an open space for market trade, or lined up in orderly ranks alongside the main road. Major settlements and trading centres were usually protected from Welsh

raids by a bank and ditch, but in time such modest defences grew into something more substantial. High stone walls, flanking towers and strong gateways not only protected the settlement from attack, but served as collection points for tolls and taxes. The towns of Abergavenny, Aberystwyth, Brecon, Cardiff, Haverfordwest, Hay-on-Wye, Monmouth and Swansea may have lost their defences to post-medieval modernisation, but their outlines can usually be detected from the air, fossilised into the townscape by later roads and property boundaries. Cowbridge, Chepstow, Pembroke and particularly Tenby (Fig. 6.13), retain substantial portions of the old walls, while the fortified plantation towns of Caernarfon, Conwy and Denbigh – first laid down in the 1280s by Edward I to encourage English colonisation at the expense of the dispossessed Welsh – preserve virtually intact defensive circuits.

Although a few of the present-day towns can claim a native origin, most owe their growth to the Anglo-Norman invaders; but since the

Welsh economy was largely based on agriculture, it is perhaps unsurprising that the majority of rural native settlements consisted of individual farmsteads and small hamlets, widely scattered through the countryside.

For most people at this time, life was short, hard and utterly devoid of the essentials and comforts we now take for granted. Few ever travelled beyond their immediate locality. Food was grown and produced on the farm, water came from the nearest stream or spring, and firewood was gathered from the forest. Gerald of Wales (d.1223) wrote that the Welsh do not build great stone houses, but 'content themselves with wattled huts on the edges of the forest, put up with little labour or expense, but strong enough to last a year or two'.

With such simple and easily constructed dwellings, and lacking the infrastructure we now take for granted, it was relatively easy to 'up sticks' and move to a more amenable location should environmental conditions change for the worse. The climate had been steadily improving since Roman times, so that it was once more viable to resettle upland areas; but as the fourteenth century dawned there was a sudden downturn, heralding a period called the 'Little Ice Age'. Europe suffered terrible famines, and before the population levels could recover an even worse disaster took place – the pandemic known to history as the Black Death. It is estimated that as much as 60% of the population died in the years 1348–49 alone, and further intermittent outbreaks occurred over the next three centuries.

Once again the remoter settlements and farmsteads were abandoned as unprofitable, except for occasional summer use. It was a process of ebb and flow that has at least enabled the archaeological remains to survive relatively unchanged in the uplands, in contrast to more fertile lands where they have been obliterated by subsequent agriculture and modern developments. The remains of abandoned farmsteads and deserted medieval villages (DMVs for short) can be found all over the countryside of Wales (Figs 6.60–6.68). The reasons for abandonment are not always known, and plague may not have been the sole culprit. In fact, some upland sites may have been deserted in relatively recent times, either because the soil had become worked out, or the prospect of employment in the growing industrialised towns proved a more attractive existence.

The majority of peasant houses dating from this time survive only as meagre foundations, and their elongated layout has given rise to the generic term **long-huts** (which also serves to distinguish them from the much earlier roundhouses of the Bronze and Iron Ages). They are often called 'longhouses', but this term, strictly speaking, relates to their *function* as much as their shape, since a longhouse accommodated people and livestock under the same

Fig. 6.14 The drystone ruins of long-huts in Cwm Brwynog

TOP: **Fig. 6.15a** A platform house on Gelligaer Common, as it appears today; BOTTOM: **6.15b** The house as it might have looked

roof. No doubt many long-huts were used in this way, but others may have been purely domestic, the cattle being penned in an adjacent building.

As mentioned above, the physical remains of long-huts range from innocuous earthworks to stony ruins, depending on the choice of available building materials. Paradoxically, the good preservation of a site might be indicative of a relatively recent date, and what might look like the foundations of a typical medieval long-hut could in fact be the remains of a derelict post-medieval cottage. Without archaeological investigation it is usually very difficult to put an exact date to such fragmentary remains, let alone decide if they might represent a permanent settlement, or were just temporarily occupied during the summer months.

Such was the case at Ynys Ettws, a pair of stone-built long-huts situated in a sheltered hollow beside the A4086 road as it winds through the dramatic Llanberis Pass. One of the huts was excavated by the Gwynedd Archaeological Trust and was found to have consisted of a single room, measuring 8m by 3.2m with a central hearth. Evidence from radiocarbon dating suggests it was occupied from at least 1260, and that the landscape was more heavily wooded than it now appears. However, the drystone walls that can be seen today are the result of rebuilding and reoccupation in the 1650s. A group of almost identical buildings on the other side of the mountain range at Cwm Brwynog, on the westerly slopes of Eryri, have been identified as the *hafod* settlement of '*Crombroinok*' mentioned in early fourteenth-century documents. A hafod was a temporary dwelling used by herders when the cattle were taken to the high pastures for summer grazing. This practice of summer migration was still being carried out here in the nineteenth century, so it is likely that these ruinous buildings were used over a long period of time and were repaired or rebuilt when necessary.

Another characteristic medieval peasant building is known as a **platform house**, so-called because it was constructed on an artificially-levelled platform cut into sloping ground. The long axis of the building pointed down-slope, with the narrow end facing any water flowing downhill (a sensible precaution in a rainy upland environment). Although the actual fabric of the house has perished, the platform survives to mark its former existence. Many later hill farms were built in exactly the same fashion, and may have evolved from simpler platform buildings on the same site. Platform houses (or 'house platforms' as they are sometimes called) were first recognised as a specific type in the 1930s, when several were investigated on Gelligaer Common in Glamorgan (Figs 6.15a & 6.15b). Finds suggested an occupation period in the late-thirteenth and early-fourteenth century.

The largest and most impressive group of platforms in Wales can be seen at Bailey Bedw, just north of St Harmon near Rhayader (Fig. 6.61). Free of obscuring undergrowth and particularly prominent in early morning sunlight, the hillside is pockmarked with around 15 house platforms, overlain by the more obvious outlines of a later farmstead. Some of the platforms were occupied in the fifteenth and sixteenth centuries, perhaps even into the 1600s.

Gerald's comment about 'wattled huts' is probably something of an exaggeration (unless he was describing the hovels that the very poorest members of society had to subsist in). He seems to be referring to timber-framed buildings with walls of wattle and daub panels, which were once a common feature of the Welsh countryside, but that now survive mainly in mid Wales and the Marches. However, most timber-framed houses are quite substantial constructions and could certainly last far longer than 'a year or two'. The oldest ones still standing today date back to the early-fifteenth century, and probably represent a period of replacement and rebuilding after the widespread devastation caused by the Glyndŵr rebellion.

Throughout the medieval period, the almost universal form of dwelling was based on the **hall** – a large multi-purpose room rising to a lofty roof

Fig. 6.16 Cutaway reconstruction through a typical medieval hall-house (based on Maestorglwyd near Hay-on-Wye, which has been recently dated to c.1412)

space, with an open hearth burning on the floor (Fig. 6.16). The fire was used for cooking as well as for heating, while daylight filtered in through unglazed windows. Those of a higher social standing could afford grander halls, with the luxury of window glass, as well as a suite of more private chambers at one end of the building. They might even choose to surround their home with a water-filled ditch (Figs 6.69 & 6.70) to form what is termed a **moated site** or homestead moat. Unlike castles, the purpose of the moat was more to do with status rather than defence (though it would be handy in deterring opportunistic thieves and cattle raiders). Moats needed a ready supply of water to keep the ditches topped up, so they were usually located on low-lying, boggy ground. They are far more common in England, particularly in the Midlands and East Anglia, but there is a dense concentration east of Wrexham where the flat lands of the Maelor district jut into the Shropshire plains.

Fig. 6.17 Interior of the hall at the Bishop's Palace at Lamphey

folk were modified or replaced by more permanent buildings that featured enclosed fireplaces and chimneys, and rooms on two or more floors. The origin of the modern house can be traced back to this period, as the smoky open hall that had for so long been the norm, was transformed into buildings that the reader, some four centuries on, might recognise as 'home'.

Those even further up the pecking order could invest in more substantial dwellings with stone walls and mural fireplaces, perhaps even with accommodation on two floors rather than one, such as Tretower Court (Fig. 6.71) and Old Beaupre manor house (Fig. 6.73). Grandest of all are the aristocratic houses such as the Bishop's Palaces at St Davids and Lamphey (Fig. 6.17). Now echoing shells, they were built on a scale that blatantly displayed the power and wealth enjoyed by certain medieval churchmen.

But that luxury was not to last forever. As we have already seen, the sixteenth century witnessed sweeping changes to the social, religious and economic life of the country. Monasteries were pulled down and castles were left to fall into ruin. The nobility now chose to spend their money on building ostentatious mansions that, ironically, incorporated features that formerly adorned their ancestral strongholds. Even in the houses of the lower classes an architectural revolution was taking place, as the impermanent dwellings of the country

All three of these Glamorgan sites evolved from twelfth-century 'ringwork' castles, and the circular shape of the original defences still shows through the later masonry.

LEFT: **Fig. 6.18 Ogmore** (SS 882 769) retains an early keep (see also Fig. 6.1) and guarded a crossing-point on the river, now marked by a row of stepping stones.

ABOVE LEFT: **Fig. 6.19 Coity** (SS 923 815) is a few miles away. The castle was needed to protect the northern approaches from Welsh-held territories.

ABOVE: **Fig. 6.20 Bridgend** (SS 901 801) lies between the two, and is believed to have been expensively rebuilt in stone by King Henry II when under temporary royal control.

Figs 6.21a & 6.21b Chepstow Castle (ST 534 942). Another view of Chepstow Castle, this time from the impregnable river frontage at high tide. The early-Norman keep (see also Fig. 5.26) is visible to the right, with later buildings extending along the cliff edge to the left. The defences of Chepstow were greatly enhanced during the thirteenth century, while the domestic accommodation was upgraded to meet the changing needs of the castle-owning aristocracy, ever into the seventeenth century. The view (left) shows the elongated outline of the castle from the south-west, with the meandering course of the River Wye beyond.

Fig. 6.22 Manorbier Castle (SN 298 504). This fine castle on the south Pembrokeshire coast shows many phases of alteration and extension, as the owners found enough resources to embark on a new phase of building work. Although most of the structure dates from the thirteenth century, there is an early twelfth-century hall embedded in the cluster of buildings at the furthest end of the site. Manorbier was the home of the De Barri family and the birthplace (c.1146) of Gerald de Barri, more familiarly known as the cleric and historian Gerald of Wales (*Giraldis Cambrensis*). Gerald referred to his birthplace in glowing terms, calling it a fortified house rather than a proper castle, and nestling in a pleasant bay with a fish pond, orchard and a watermill close by. The ruins of a much later mill and dovecote can just be glimpsed in the background, while the long building in the foreground is a post-medieval barn, taking up much of what was the outer ward of the castle.

Fig. 6.23 Pembroke Castle (SM 981 015). When the Normans arrived in Pembrokeshire in 1093 they chose this rocky ridge as the location for one of their principal castles. The 'fortress of wooden stakes and turf' described by Gerald of Wales was to grow into one of the largest and strongest castles in the country. This view shows the twin courtyards of the castle in the foreground, with the town stretching away eastwards along the ridge. Some of the walls and towers that protected the town survive in places. Significant building work was carried out in the thirteenth century by William Marshal and his heirs, to serve as the seat of the earldom and a suitable embarkation point for conquests overseas in Ireland. Marshal was responsible for adding the enormous round keep visible in the centre of the photo (one of the largest in Britain), which contains five floors of accommodation and stands almost 80ft high. It was to prove a highly influential design among the Marcher lords of the south.

Figs 6.24a & 6.24b Carew Castle (SM 045 036). Carew lies only a few miles away from Pembroke, on another inlet of the mighty Cleddau river. As can be appreciated from these views, the castle is remarkably well-preserved – a legacy of the long and relatively peaceful years of occupation, from the twelfth century through to the seventeenth. Fortunately, the Civil War cannons did relatively little damage to Carew when compared to other castles. The view above was taken on a frosty October morning looking west across the site to a tidal corn mill in the background. The curved bay with large windows on the right is a relic of the time when the old fortress was converted into an elegant Elizabethan mansion.

Figs 6.25a & 6.25b Caldicot Castle (ST 486 885). The round keep of Pembroke proved to be an influential design that was adopted by other Marcher lords during the early thirteenth century. Here at Caldicot, on the shores of the Severn estuary, the De Bohun family strengthened the timber motte-and-bailey defences with stonework, including a fine round keep (foreground). Though not as large as the one at Pembroke, it still served as a powerful image of Anglo-Norman domination, and enabled the surrounding land to be kept under close observation. Caldicot later passed to a scion of the royal family, and a grand new gatehouse was added by the duke of Gloucester in 1383 (right). The castle was extensively restored between 1885 and 1964.

Fig. 6.26 Cefnllys Castle, Llandrindod Wells (SO 089 615). Not all medieval castles survive in such pristine condition as Pembroke. Here on Cefnllys hill, a vast array of earthworks denotes the site of not one, but two ruined castles and a late-medieval settlement The first (foreground) was built by the Marcher baron Ralph Mortimer around 1242 to secure his claim to Welsh lands here. This was attacked and destroyed in 1262. A later truce allowed Ralph's heir, Roger Mortimer, to regain and repair the castle. However, he used this loophole to build a second, and even stronger, castle at the furthest tip of the ridge, presumably recycling materials from the ruins of the first site. Since no proper excavations have taken place here, the original appearance of both castles is entirely speculative.

Two more major castles that, like Cefnllys, have been reduced to earthworks through erosion and stone robbing.

LEFT: **Fig. 6.27 Painscastle** (SO 167 462) near Hay-on-Wye. This is a Norman motte-and-bailey expensively and quickly rebuilt in stone by King Henry III in 1231, and left to fall into decay after the Glyndŵr rebellion.

BELOW: **Fig. 6.28 Builth Wells** (SO 042 510). A wintery panorama looking north across the castle and town of Builth in the Wye Valley. The Norman fort was the subject of a significant makeover by Edward I between 1277 and 1280, but unlike the king's other castles of this period, nothing now remains above ground to indicate what it looked like.

Fig. 6.29 New Radnor (SO 216 610). Radnor was 'new' in the 1090s, when it replaced the older Welsh settlement a short distance away. The Anglo-Norman invaders carved up a natural ridge to form an impressively large castle that featured an oval inner ward (centre of the photo) with double-ditches separating it from an angular outer bailey (foreground). The defences were later rebuilt in stone with strong walls and multiple towers. New Radnor suffered frequent devastating Welsh raids, the last by Owain Glŷndwr in 1402, and while part of the castle remained in use as a prison into the seventeenth century, it thereafter fell into decay. Like Painscastle and Builth, the masonry was then robbed away so that not a scrap remains above ground today. On the plain below the hill stands the town, which also had its own defences (marked by a tree-lined ditch between the castle and the modern road).

Fig. 6.30 Penrhos Castle (SO 409 132). Penrhos lies north of Raglan and is a very odd site indeed. Historical records indicate it was caught up in a dispute between rival English lords, being built in 1248, attacked several times, before being destroyed in 1253. There is no sign of any stonework here and the date is surprisingly late for an earthwork castle. From the air it bears a marked resemblance to a fried egg. The mound, or motte, is centrally placed within the bailey, instead of to the side, as usual. There are fainter earthworks in the same field that hint that it might occupy the site of an older hillfort.

Fig. 6.31 Prestatyn Castle (SJ 072 833). Few visitors to the north Wales resort of Prestatyn will realise that the town has a castle. Only slight vestiges now remain, here picked out in low evening sunshine, looking north towards the sea. The manor had been a Norman holding since the 1080s and there are references to one Robert de Banaster building a 'tower' here in the 1160s. It may look feeble, but the castle is low-lying enough to have benefited from broad water-filled ditches designed to keep the enemy at bay, and excavation in 1913 revealed that the bailey had been walled in stone.

Fig. 6.32 Castlemartin Castle (SR 915 984). This view shows the modern village clustered beside the concentric earthworks that give the place its name. Away to the south stretches the no-go expanse of an MOD firing range. Although this is a documented medieval site, held from the lordship of Pembroke, the form of the double earthwork is much more typical of Iron Age sites (of which there are several in the neighbourhood). It is possible that the Normans simply reused a convenient hillfort when they settled this area of Wales.

Fig. 6.33 Llawhaden Castle (SN 073 175). In another part of Pembrokeshire, the bishops of St Davids established a castle to safeguard their lands here. The deep ditch of the original ringwork is still clearly visible in the photo (left) taken from the north and, like Castlemartin, it may have evolved from an earlier hillfort. However, Llawhaden was important enough to warrant an expensive rebuild during the late-thirteenth and fourteenth centuries, when stone walls, towers and comfortable apartments (by medieval standards at least) were provided for the use of the bishops and visiting dignitaries. A market town was also established, stretching away along the road out of shot to the right.

Fig. 6.34 Montgomery Castle (SO 221 968). Montgomery was started in 1223 to replace a nearby earthwork castle of strategic importance on the English-Welsh border (see Fig. 5.22). The king's advisor, Hubert de Burgh, identified an ideal site to build a new royal fortress. The defences consisted of a series of walled enclosures along a rocky ridge the innermost forming a compact courtyard with a twin-towered gatehouse. The design proved to be highly influential, and the finished castle successfully resisted several Welsh attacks. In the 1620s an 'elegant and noble' mansion was built in the outer ward. Sadly this, along with the rest of the castle, was slighted during the English Civil War. This view looks south-east across the castle rock and the existing town of Montgomery beyond.

Hubert de Burgh (d.1243) was a castle builder of some significance in the Welsh Marches. Aside from Montgomery, he also rebuilt the Three Castles of Gwent (Grosmont, Skenfrith and White Castle) after receiving that lordship in 1201. Work took place over an extended period of time and reportedly cost Hubert an 'infinite amount of money' before he fell from grace and was deprived of his lands in 1232.

Fig. 6.35 White Castle (SO 379 167). This view looks south-east over the clustered towers and water-filled moat of the castle. Like many early thirteenth-century designs, the castle featured one or more walled enclosures with rounded flanking towers projecting out to face any attacking force (see chapter frontispiece).

Figs 6.36a & 6.36b Llansteffan Castle (SN 352 101). Llansteffan was one of three castles built by the Norman invaders to control water-borne traffic using the estuaries of the Tywi, Taf and Gwendraeth rivers in Carmarthenshire. Utilising a prominent headland above the sea, the first castle was a simple ringwork within the remains of an Iron Age hillfort. Over time the defences were rebuilt piecemeal in stone, including the twin-towered gatehouse (left).

LEFT: **Fig. 6.37 Laugharne Castle** (SN 301 107). This nearby castle is less dramatically situated than Llansteffan. It not only guarded a river crossing but a small adjoining town as well, and remained in occupation well into Elizabethan times. It was finally humbled by cannon fire in the English Civil War. This low view shows the imposing river frontage from the south.

BELOW: **Fig. 6.38 Kidwelly** (SN 409 070). This is a high view from the north, of the last of the triumvirate of castles. A massive scheme of rebuilding occurred during the thirteenth and fourteenth centuries, yet still respecting the curving line of the original timber fort founded around 1106 by the Bishop of Salisbury in order to protect his gifted lands here.

The castles of the native rulers of Wales may have been less ambitious than their Anglo-Norman rivals, but they were cleverly designed to take advantage of the natural landscape in order to defend the main routes through the upland territcries.

TOP LEFT: **Fig. 6.39 Dolbadarn** (SH 587 598). The round tower of Dolbadarn Castle, built by Llywelyn the Great in the early thirteenth century to protect the difficult pass through the mountains of Eryri.

ABOVE: **Fig. 6.40 Dolwyddelan** (SH 722 521). This is another of Llywelyn's towers. The pristine condition of the battlements is due to nineteenth-century restoration work.

LEFT: **Fig. 6.41 Criccieth** (SH 499 376). Llywelyn also built the coastal stronghold of Criccieth Castle, which featured an impressive twin-towered gatehouse, now the most substantial part of the castle. Later works were carried out after Criccieth fell to the English in 1283.

Fig. 6.42 Castell y Bere (SH 668 086). It wasn't only Anglo-Norman aggression that the Welsh princes had to contend with, but the rivalry of their own countrymen as well. Llywelyn the Great even faced a rebellion by one of his sons, so that in 1221 he had to raise an army and build a castle to keep the peace. Here in the Dysynni Valley, the Welsh masons began constructing one of the largest and most ambitious native castles, featuring an elaborate gateway and variously shaped towers scattered across an almost unassailable rocky eminence. Two of the towers were elongated D-shaped in plan, a particular favourite design of native castle builders. One can be seen in the foreground. This view looks north-east across the castle rock to the heights of Cadair Idris, one of the highest mountain ranges in Wales.

Fig. 6.43 Caerphilly Castle (ST 156 871). In 1268 the powerful and wealthy Marcher lord Gilbert de Clare began building Caerphilly to negate the Welsh threat to his lands in Glamorgan. The sheer scale of the castle reveals how seriously he took that threat. Work continued for the next 30 or so years, resulting in the complex concentric fortress visible above, in a view looking east across the innermost citadel. The plan was effectively one line of defence within another, with a series of moats and lakes to keep enemy siege machines at bay. The whole site encompasses 25 acres, making it one of the largest medieval castles in Britain. The concentric design was to reach its peak with King Edward's castles in north Wales (see Figs 6.47–6.50). However, the impressive present-day appearance of Caerphilly is very much due to a lengthy restoration carried out in 1928–39, which saw many of the ruined walls rebuilt from the ground up, and the moats later re-flooded.

Figs 6.44a & **6.44b Carreg Cennen Castle** (SN 667 191). The original Welsh castle here was completely rebuilt after it was captured by the English in 1283, and remained in use until 1462 when it was purposely demolished. The view right shows the north front of the castle, with massed towers, entrance ramp and foundations of the outer ward, all designed to prevent attackers from breaking in to the central courtyard. However, when viewed from another angle (above), the natural strength of the site becomes immediately apparent. The sheer limestone crag rendered it impervious to attack from the south flank. Crowning a limestone rock high above the valley, with the Black Mountains as a backdrop, Carreg Cennen must arguably be the most dramatically sited castle in Wales. Historical facts may be scarce, but numerous legends have grown up about the castle's past and its occupants. An unusual feature of the site is a deep cave that was incorporated into the medieval defences, and which can be explored along a passageway from the courtyard.

Fig. 6.45 **Flint Castle** (SJ 247 733). Flint was among the first castles that King Edward I built to tame the native princes. Groundwork began in 1277 and the building was largely complete by 1286. The design was superficially simple (as can be seen from this aerial view looking north-west across the site), but the most striking feature was the detached round keep in the foreground, thought to have been inspired by the castles Edward would have seen on his travels on the Continent. This has an unusually complex layout, with passages connecting a series of small rooms ranged around a central chamber. In 1301 the now-lost upper floor was crowned with 'a noble and beautiful circular gallery', which Fig. 6.4 attempts to visualise.

Fig. 6.46 **Hawarden Castle** (SJ 319 654), located nearby, also has a round keep of unusual plan, probably modelled on Flint.

Fig. 6.47 Rhuddlan Castle (SJ 025 779). As work progressed on Flint in the summer of 1277, Edward's masons travelled west to the River Clwyd, where there was already an existing motte-and-bailey castle. Ignoring this, the builders started to construct a new stone fortress to an innovative concentric plan, whereby the innermost enclosure was surrounded by a series of outer defensive lines. The castle was largely complete by 1280 when the towers were roofed, although further work on the internal timber buildings continued for some years. This view looks west across the diamond-shaped inner ward with its round towers and paired gatehouses. Surrounding this was a more irregularly-shaped outer ward, and then an encircling ditch that connected with a fortified dock so that supplies could be brought into the castle even if the surrounding countryside was under hostile control.

Figs 6.48a & 6.48b Harlech Castle (SH 581 312). After Prince Llywelyn was killed in 1282, Edward pushed on with his plan of subjugating the Welsh, and here on the rock of Harlech another substantial fortress was built between 1283 and 1289. Like Rhuddlan, it had a concentric plan where the strongly-defended inner ward was enclosed by a lower outer circuit of walls. The rock gave excellent protection on most sides and, at the time it was built, it was lapped by the sea, so that supplies could be brought to the castle by boat. Harlech has arguably the most spectacular setting of all the Edwardian castles in Wales, and the above view looks north over the massive walls and towers towards the distant snow-topped peaks of Eryri.

Figs **6.49a** & **6.49b** Conwy **Castle** (SH 784 774). Both Conwy Castle and Caernarfon Castle (overleaf) were built in the aftermath of King Edward's wars against Llywelyn. Both featured curtain walls studded with numerous towers – round in the case of Conwy, but of more elaborate multangular plan at Caernarfon. The unusual and costly design of the latter may have been intended to recall the glories of imperial Roman architecture. Like other Edwardian castles they could be supplied by sea and had defended towns adjoining them, to encourage English settlers at the expense of the ousted Welsh. The town walls of both castles are exceptionally well-preserved.

Figs 6.50a & **6.50b Caernarfon Castle** (SH 478 627). Another view of the castle and walled town of Caernarfon, looking west across the grid system of the medieval settlement sheltering within a protective *enceinte* studded with towers and gateways. The River Seiont and the Menai Strait (in full flood in the above view) gave much-needed natural protection to the low-lying site, and in addition the Cadnant stream (now culverted over) flowed around the walls. Despite these formidable defences, the Welsh broke into Caernarfon in 1294, and embarked on an orgy of violence and destruction. The hated sheriff was strung up, the unfinished castle was ransacked and everything combustible was set ablaze. Costly repairs were begun when the English recovered possession the following year, and although the works continued until 1330, parts of the castle were never fully completed to plan.

Fig. 6.51 Beaumaris Castle, Anglesey (SH 607 762). This was the last of Edward's castles in Wales, began in 1295 after a violent, but short-lived uprising, that saw the incomplete Caernarfon torched. To end any further unrest, Beaumaris was ambitiously planned on a concentric layout of almost geometrical perfection – but it was never finished: cutbacks and costs left the castle with neatly planed-off walls and towers. The above view looks south over the castle to the Menai Strait and the uplands of Eryri, lit by the low winter sun.

Fig. 6.52 Raglan Castle (SO 414 083). Raglan was the last major castle to be built in Wales and is also one of best-preserved – even a savage mauling by Parliamentary cannon fire in the English Civil War has not entirely robbed Raglan of its former glory. In this view looking east across the site, the distinctive and attractive use of multangular towers is apparent. The large tower to the left and the smaller ones visible to the right and in the background date to a major rebuilding of the original medieval manor in the 1460s. Right at the back can be glmpsed the hexagonal Great Tower, which is set within its own defensive moat beyond the castle walls. This was one of the first buildings to be raised, probably in the 1430s, while the prominent block of buildings in the centre was among the last – an addition of Tudor times that included an enormous banqueting hall and a long gallery on the upper floor, a prerequisite of any great house of the time.

Fig. 6.53 Powis Castle, Welshpool
(SJ 215 064). Powis is also known as Castell Coch ('Red Castle') from the colour of the original stonework. A thirteenth-century stronghold of the Welsh rulers of Powys, the castle passed to the Herbert family in 1587 who began the transformation into the palatial residence visible today. Still the seat of the earls of Powis, the castle is maintained by the National Trust. This view looks north across the elegant terraced gardens to the town of Welshpool in the distance.

Fig. 6.54 St Donat's Castle (SS 934 680). St Donats originally featured a twelfth-century keep and curtain wall, with an added outer ring creating a concentric layout. It was the seat of the Stradling family from about 1300 (despite falsely claiming that they were among the original Norman conquerors of Glamorgan). The last heir was killed in a duel in 1738, and thereafter the castle deteriorated. Some modest repairs were carried out during the nineteenth and early twentieth centuries, but then in 1925 the American newspaper tycoon William Randolph Hearst acquired St Donats and embarked on a vigorous (and highly controversial) restoration, even adding buildings from elsewhere into the mix. The castle now forms part of Atlantic College.

Fig. 6.55 Abergavenny (SO 298 141). Many of the existing towns in Wales owe their origin to the Anglo-Norman invaders in the eleventh and twelfth centuries, who were keen to stabilise their conquests with the economic benefits of market trade. Although Abergavenny occupies the site of a Roman fort, it was the Norman castle (foreground) that served as the impetus for its subsequent growth as a key Marcher town. The timber defences of the motte-and-bailey were later replaced in stone, although the little battlemented tower on the right is a Georgian folly that now houses the town museum. The walls that once defended the town have been lost to post-medieval growth, and the twelfth-century Benedictine priory buildings fell victim to Henry VIII's religious reforms. However, the church itself (centre of picture) is still largely complete and contains a magnificent collection of medieval monuments. This view looks north-east over the castle and town to the distant hump of Ysgyryd Fawr on the horizon.

Figs 6.56a & **6.56b Brecon** (SO 046 288). Pushing west from Abergavenny, the Normans plundered the Welsh kingdom of Brycheiniog in the 1090s, and established a castle on a defensible site where the Honddu joins the Usk. The castle can be seen as a triangle of land in the centre of the photo below, which shows Brecon from the east. Trees cover much of the site, and most of the old buildings have been incorporated into more modern constructions. Close by stands the Cathedral Church of St John (right), which mainly dates from the early thirteenth century. Founded as a Benedictine priory, possibly on a pre-Norman Welsh site, it became a cathedral with the creation of the diocese in 1923. The town itself was established on the east bank of the Honddu (foreground, below) and in time was protected from Welsh raids by walls, towers and gates, now alas lost to urban growth.

Figs 6.57a & **6.57b Hay-on-Wye** (SO 230 422). Renowned for its numerous bookshops and cultural festivals, the Marcher town of Hay stands right on the border with England, huddled about the remains of its imposing castle. This strategic military base was established in the 1070s and, unsurprisingly, became a frequent target for Welsh animosity. Parts of the medieval fabric still survive, but the most obvious feature is the grand mansion built over the ruins in around 1640, which has recently undergone a £5.5 million scheme of restoration. To the left is a view of the southern façade of the house, showing the twelfth-century keep (originally the gateway into the castle), and beside it the arched opening of a later entrance.

Figs 6.58a, 6.58b & 6.58c Cardigan (SN 178 460). Cardigan was another important Norman settlement, but one that fell under Welsh control for long periods of time. In 1171 Lord Rhys of Deheubarth rebuilt the castle in stone and held the first recorded Eisteddfod here in 1176. In the thirteenth century the castle was recovered by the English and became the seat of royal power in Ceredigion. Opposite is a general view from the south, showing the bridge over the Teifi and the main street stretching northwards in a gentle curve. Above is a close-up of the castle site and the recently-restored Georgian house within the courtyard. The church of St Mary (left) served both the parish and a small Benedictine priory, of which the only remaining trace is thought to be the elaborately-decorated chancel.

Figs 6.59a, 6.59b & 6.59c Tenby (SN 135 004). This historic walled town owes its origins to the Norman invaders who established a castle here around 1100 on a naturally-defended promontory jutting into the sea (opposite, bottom). This protected a small harbour that enabled Tenby to thrive as a trading port for centuries. The town grew up on the headland above the castle, and by late medieval times was full of fine, stone merchant's houses (of which, sadly, very few survived nineteenth-century redevelopment). After repeated Welsh attacks, the simple timber defences of the town were replaced piecemeal in stone during the fourteenth and fifteenth centuries. This can be seen above as a right-angled wall studded with towers, nipping off a strip of the headland. The tall spire of St Mary's Church is visible, as is the only surviving town gate, now known as the Five Arches (above, and see Fig. 6.13).

Fig. 6.60 St Athan Deserted Medieval Village (DMV) (ST 023 682). Not all settlements endured and outgrew their humble medieval origins. Some dwindled and declined for various reasons, and here in the Vale of Glamorgan can be seen the exceptionally well-preserved vestiges of one such failure. The fields east of the modern village and parish church of St Athan are scarred with the remains of a lost settlement, here highlighted by the low January sun. The embanked trench crossing the photo diagonally marks the line of the street, flanked on the right-hand side by an orderly row of rectangles indicating the site of cottages. Each dwelling typically has a long and narrow garden plot running behind.

Fig. 6.61 Bailey Bedw DMV, St Harmon (SN 997 735). Bailey Bedw is one of the best-preserved platform house settlements in Wales. In this view (taken from the north), the medieval houses appear as subtle indentations in the slopes, partly overlain by the more obvious remains of a later farmstead. Evidently, this was home to a small farming community before being consolidated into one main holding in post-medieval times. In 1961–2 three of the platforms were excavated, and found to comprise simple turf-walled houses, one with stone foundations. From the pottery fragments recovered, it was considered that these dwellings had been occupied during the fifteenth and sixteenth centuries, perhaps even into the early 1600s. As the archaeologists found no post holes to support a roof, it seems likely that the upper part of each house was cruck-framed. They may therefore have had timber-panelled walls and been much more substantial structures than the meagre vestiges imply.

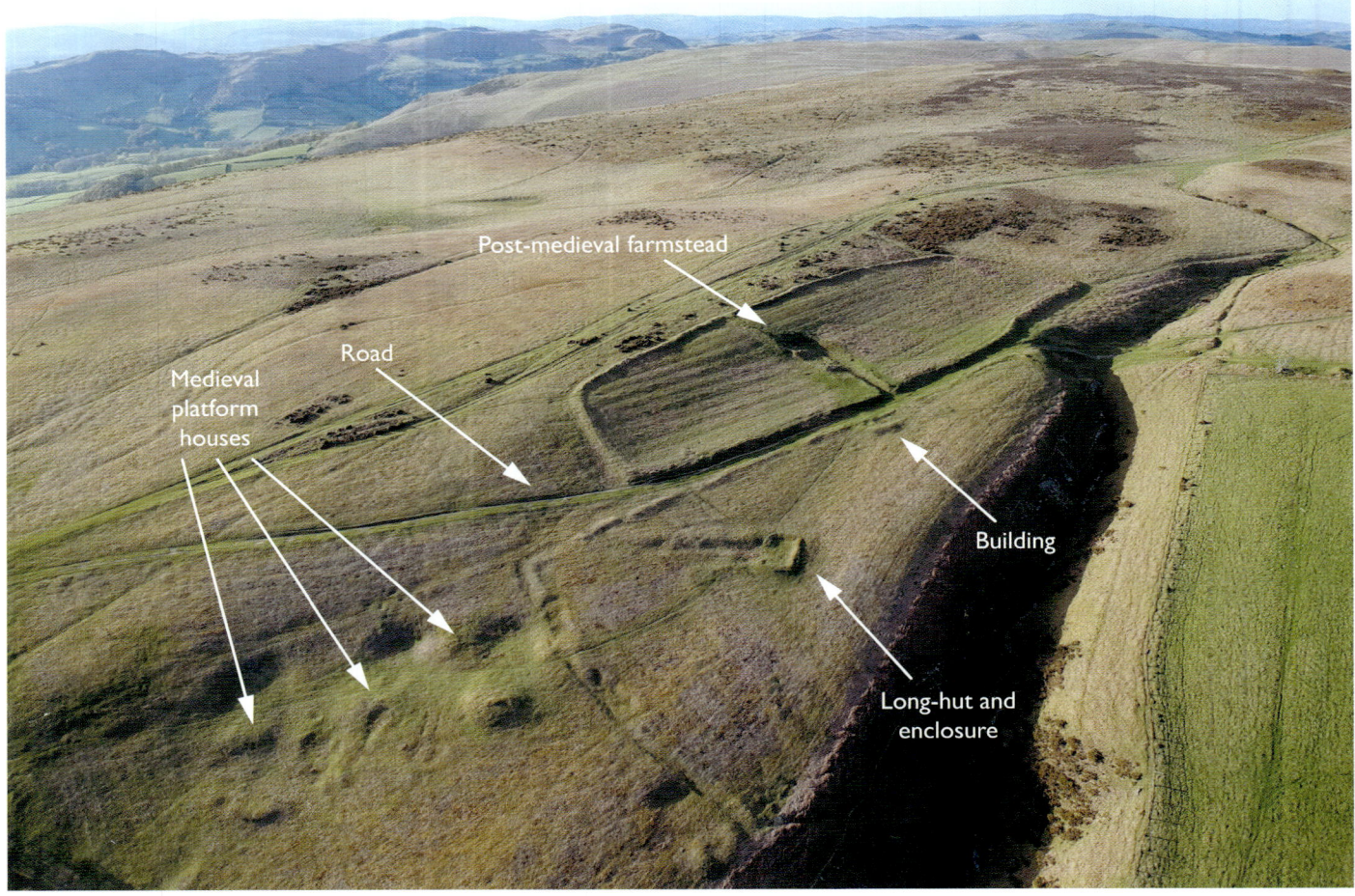

Medieval platform houses

Road

Post-medieval farmstead

Building

Long-hut and enclosure

Fig. 6.62 Aberedw Hill DMV, Builth Wells (SO 083 501). This fine group of abandoned dwellings can be found on open access land high above the Wye Valley, reached by a steep path up from the B4567, south of Llanfaredd hamlet. As interpreted in this view looking north, the earthworks include subtle house platforms, the corduroy pattern of ploughing and the stony foundations of more substantial buildings, indicative of an extended period of use. The most prominent feature here is the oval enclosure with a central building, which is likely to be a post-medieval farmstead established on marginal land outside the limits of the pre-existing cultivated fields. It would have taken a very determined and hardy family to eke out a living at such a remote upland location as this.

Far more commonplace than the nucleated settlements shown in the previous pages, are the remains of individual rural farmsteads, like these examples in upland Powys.

TOP LEFT: **Fig. 6.63 Fron Top near Llanbadarn Fynydd** (SO 117 791). The outline of a two-room house is clearly defined in the centre of the photo. There are more house sites and a possible ringwork castle further along the hill, suggesting this was an abortive medieval settlement.

ABOVE: **Fig. 6.64 Cefn Golau ridge north of Rhayader** (SN 970 733). The outline of an abandoned farmstead on the ridge.

LEFT: **Fig. 6.65 Moelfre Hill near Llanbister** (SO 117 761). This is a very well-preserved site. Each house is surrounded by varying sized gardens and paddocks, that would probably have been topped with hedges or wattled fences to keep the livestock safe and contained.

Figs 6.66a & **6.66b Penlandoppa DMV, Pontrhydfendigaid** (SN 764 663). One of several abandoned farmsteads in the hills east of Strata Florida. It was first recorded in 1546 and may have evolved out of one of the abbey's upland granges. It was still inhabited as late as 1843. Earthworks now define the embanked gardens and central longhouse, which would have been shared by both people and cattle.

Figs **6.67a** & **6.67b** Egryn DMV, Barmouth (SH 603 203). The stony landscape of Ardudwy is dotted with ruined buildings of all ages, including this well-preserved farmstead on the slopes above the National Trust-owned Egryn Abbey. Like Penlandoppa, it consists of a central longhouse with at least one outbuilding, and stands within a network of stone-walled gardens and paddocks. It is presumably of medieval date, though the relatively good condition of the remains suggests it continued to be inhabited into post-Reformation times as well. Both drawings are shown from the same angle as the photos, giving an idea of how the sites might have looked originally.

Fig. 6.68 Cyfannedd DMV, Arthog (SH 631 128). Situated in the foothills of the Cadair Idris range, this abandoned settlement consists of walled fields and at least four stone-built structures. Some were probably houses; the rest agricultural outbuildings. Like many such sites, it lies on marginal land beyond the boundaries of the existing farmsteads, suggesting post-medieval retrenchment to more manageable and better-drained soil lower down the valley. This view looks north across the site to the Mawddach estuary and coastal town of Barmouth. The long dark line of a wooden railway viaduct (opened in 1867) can be seen crossing the water.

LEFT: **Fig. 6.69 Tregynon Moat** (SO 097 983). In a field beside this Powys village is a good example of this class of medieval monument. The timber-framed house that once stood upon the island has long vanished, and only the dried-up ditches remain to mark its position.

BELOW: **Fig. 6.70 Moated site at Gadlas, Ellesmere** (SJ 372 371). Another fine moat is located just over the border in England, where such sites are found in abundance. The ditch is still partly flooded, and a supply leat can be seen extending from the lower right corner of the island to the curving line of a former stream.

Fig. 6.71 Tretower Castle and Court (SO 186 213). In contrast to the modest moats shown on the previous page, this panoramic view of Tretower shows what the nobility could accomplish given sufficient money. This fine group of medieval buildings was occupied successively for over 700 years, starting with the twelfth- and thirteenth-century castle in the background. In the foreground is its successor, a grand courtyard house predominately dating from the mid fifteenth century. The gatehouse and battlemented wall gave it the appearance, if not the reality, of a strongly fortified dwelling. Both sites are in the care of Cadw, and the interior of the hall has been lavishly fitted out as it would have looked in medieval times.

Fig. 6.72 Lamphey Bishop's Palace (SN 018 009). The great wealth harvested by the Church is reflected in the palaces that the Bishops of St Davids built for themselves at Lamphey near Pembroke, and at the Cathedral City itself (Fig. 6.98). In the background can be seen a succession of lavishly-appointed halls dating from 1200 to 1350, and which would have been approached through the gate tower, now standing in isolation in the foreground.

Fig. 6.73 Old Beaupre (ST 009 721) is a similar statement in stone, but built by the secular Basset family of Glamorgan. The core of the building dates to the 1300s, but it was extended and refurbished in Elizabethan times when many of the finer dressed-stone details were added.

Fig. 6.74 Llwyncelyn, Cwmyoy (SO 309 217). Llwyncelyn is an exceptionally well-preserved medieval hall, hidden away in the Black Mountains near Abergavenny. It was built in about 1420 by a well-to-do landowner in the aftermath of the Glyndŵr rebellion, and has recently been restored by the Landmark Trust. It features a stone hall with a parlour cross-wing at the upper end. Both were originally open to the ornate roof and heated by open hearths, although in the seventeenth century enclosed fireplaces and upper floors were added in an effort to 'modernise' the medieval house.

ABOVE **Fig. 6.75 Llangelynnin, Conwy** (SH 752 737). Seemingly forgotten by the world, this remotely situated church was in regular use until 1840, but now only the occasional service is held here. The ancient-looking building dates from the twelfth to the fifteenth centuries, and probably occupies the site of an earlier church dedicated to the sixth-century St Celynnin. The saint's holy well is built into the boundary wall on the lower right side.

LEFT: **Fig. 6.76 Pennant Melangell, Llangynog** (SJ 024 265). Located in a tranquil valley in Powys, this restored twelfth-century church stands within a circular graveyard ringed with ancient yews. Pilgrims journeyed to this remote spot to visit the shrine of the seventh-century St Melangell. Although it was destroyed at the Reformation, surviving fragments enabled archaeologists to reconstruct the shrine in 1989. The unusual apsidal chancel (right-hand end) was rebuilt from the original footings at the same time.

Fig. 6.77 St Dwynwen's Church, Anglesey (SH 387 627). Dwynwen lived in fifth-century Brecon, but having been crossed in love, she retired to spend her days as a hermit on this remote island. She became known as the patron saint of lovers and her feast day (25 January) is now celebrated as a Welsh equivalent of St Valentine's Day. This view looks north across Llanddwyn Island towards the dark canopy of Newborough Forest on the mainland. Her simple church has been rebuilt many times. The existing cruciform ruin dates to c.1500, but excavations in 2021 revealed the foundations of the simpler buildings that preceded it.

Fig. 6.78 Llangwyfan, Anglesey (SH 336 683). When St Cwyfan's church was built in the twelfth century, it stood on a low headland jutting into Caernarfon Bay, but coastal erosion over the centuries has had a dramatic effect on the land around it. The existing retaining wall was built in 1893 to try to prevent further damage from the relentless waves, and now the church can only be reached on foot across a rocky causeway at low tide.

Not all churches outlasted the medieval period. The Protestant reforms of the sixteenth century witnessed the closure of many shrines and places of pilgrimage. Social changes and population migration had its effect as well.

ABOVE: **Fig. 6.79 Capel Lligwy** (SH 498 864) stands alone in an Anglesey field, with no sign of the village it must have once served.

TOP RIGHT: **Fig. 6.80 Llanbad** (SS 994 853). This mountain-top church fell into disuse in Victorian times with the decline of upland farming in this area of Glamorgan.

RIGHT: **Fig. 6.81 St Margaret's Island** (SS 123 973), off the Tenby coast, has a complex of buildings thought to comprise a late medieval religious site. Abandoned at the Reformation, it was reoccupied and converted into cottages in the 1830s when much of the little island was quarried for limestone. In the background is the larger isle of Caldey, which has its own modern-day community of monks.

Both of these churches had a monastic origin, but they were never large or well-endowed enough to have the usual range of conventual buildings, which in any case would likely have been lost at the Reformation.

Fig. 6.82 Llangennith, Gower (SS 429 915) stands in a near-circular churchyard that suggests an early medieval foundation. The building is largely fourteenth-century in date, and is the reputed burial place of St Cenydd, whose hermitage was nearby.

Fig. 6.83 St Mary's Church, Beddgelert (SH 591 480) also had a Celtic origin, but was re-founded as an Augustinian priory in the early thirteenth century. Most of the surviving fabric dates from that time, with a hefty dose of Victorian restoration work for good measure.

The Dissolution of the Monasteries had far-reaching effects on the society, economy and religious life of Tudor Wales. ABOVE: **Fig. 6.84 Haverfordwest Priory** (SM 956 152) was founded around 1200 and closed in 1536, when anything of value was ransacked – even the very stones that made up the fabric of the building. This view, looking north, shows the excavated remains of the cloister in the foreground with the ruined church behind. To the right is a restored medieval garden. BELOW: **Figs 6.85a & 6.85b Strata Marcella, Welshpool** (SJ 251 104) is a Welsh foundation of 1170. Stone robbers have been particularly thorough in wiping all trace of this abbey off the map. The scant earthworks are interpreted in the drawing, giving some idea of the original scale of the site.

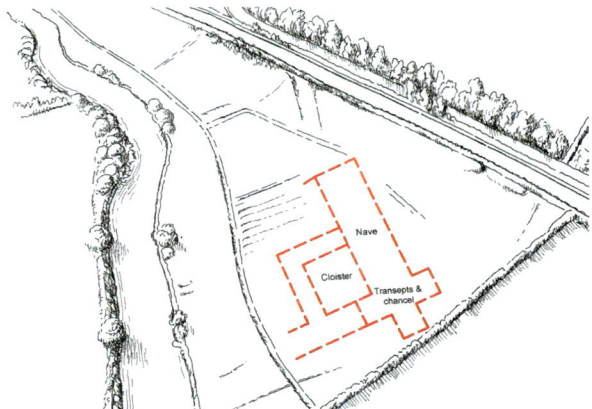

Fig. 6.86 Strata Florida, Pontrhydfendigaid (SN 747 657). A more famous native monastery was Strata Florida, known in Welsh as Ystrad Fflur ('the Vale of Flowers'). It was originally a Norman foundation, but the Cistercian abbey was generously endowed by Lord Rhys of Deheubarth and became closely associated with the native princes and their struggles for independence. Here, the Welsh chronicles were written, meetings convened between the native rulers, and royal family members laid to rest. Much of the abbey was built by 1200, but it was ransacked by English forces in the 1400s and little was left standing after 1539 – although the Romanesque west doorway (see Fig. 6.6) is a miraculous survivor. The above view looks westwards along the length of the cruciform church, its stunted walls sharply defined under a covering of snow. Ongoing excavations are revealing more of the extent of the monastic precinct and its lost buildings.

Figs **6.87a** & **6.87b** Talley Abbey (SN 633 328). Another of Rhys' generous endowments enabled the building of an abbey at Talley, near Llandovery. Work began in the 1170s and the ground plan was laid out for a typical cruciform church; however, the monks overreached themselves. What with rivalry from Whitland Abbey, political turmoil and periodic warfare, the scheme had to be curtailed. The unbuilt parts are marked out in the grass. Most of the monastic buildings are unexcavated as they lie under adjacent properties. At the Dissolution the chancel was retained for worship, until a new parish church was built in 1772 (the whitewashed building alongside).

Fig. 6.88 Penmon Priory, Anglesey
(SH 630 807). This fine group of medieval buildings lies at the easternmost tip of Anglesey, and marks the site of a Celtic monastery founded in the sixth century by St Cybi. The existing structures (seen here from the east) were built in stages during the course of the twelfth century. The disproportionately long chancel (foreground) and the claustral buildings (now ruined) were thirteenth-century additions when the site was reorganised as an Augustinian house. Penmon was a lucky survivor of the Reformation, for it was not ransacked as usual, but retained for use as a parish church. Several carved stone crosses and a holy well commemorate its early medieval predecessor.

Fig. 6.89 Ewenny Priory, Bridgend
(SS 912 778). Ewenny too, managed to outlive the Dissolution relatively unscathed, and the twelfth-century church was retained for worship. The cool, dark interior with its array of ponderous round arches, is an excellent example of the austere Romanesque style of architecture. The cruciform building can be seen at the rear of this view, looking north over the site. By 1300 a fortified wall with gates and towers had been built, giving both protection and prestige to the monastic precinct. While most of the church was preserved after 1536, the claustral buildings were converted into a large Tudor house, which in turn was replaced by the existing Georgian mansion in the foreground.

Fig. 6.90 Marcross grange, Llantwit Major (SS 926 694). Monasteries relied on obtaining food and produce from the agricultural estates they owned, and established granges (farms) to manage those lands. Marcross, in the fertile Vale of Glamorgan, is a particularly well-preserved site. In this view from the north, the low winter sun picks out a complex pattern of building platforms, fish ponds and enclosures straddling a minor road. A single upstanding fragment of a tithe barn casts a long shadow near the centre of the earthworks. Just a short distance away is another fine grange site at Monknash (Fig. 6.91), which preserves more ruined buildings. Both sites belonged to Neath Abbey.

Fig. 6.91 Neath Abbey's grange at Monknash (SS 918 706). The site is particularly obvious in this view, looking towards the south. The boundary hedges outline a roughly pentagonal enclosure of 20 acres, which contrasts with the more regular pattern of post-medieval fields spreading to the horizon. There are clear signs of further internal divisions, roadways and building sites, including the dovecote already seen in close-up (Fig. 6.10). At the far end of the enclosure a group of buildings marks the little hamlet of Monknash, with the parish church in the field beyond.

Fig. 6.92 Grangefield moat, Magor (ST 389 850). The place-name suggests this was the estate centre for the lands that Tintern Abbey owned on the Gwent Levels, the region of flat marshy ground bordering the Severn estuary. The central island is fairly obvious in this view looking west, and it lies slightly skewed within a larger outer enclosure. The moats would have been fed from the surrounding network of ditches or reens, which have been draining the Levels since Roman times.

Fig. 6.93 Llwyngwryl fishtrap (SH 582 096). Fish formed an important part of the medieval diet, and fishing rights were carefully controlled by the Church and secular landowners. This view shows a well-preserved V-shaped trap revealed by the ebbing tide on the Meirionnydd coast. A collecting pool can just be seen at the apex of the trap.

Fig. 6.94 Twyn y Gaer pillow mounds (SN 990 281). The humble rabbit was also a valued source of food in medieval times, and here on a hilltop near Brecon, can be seen a variety of cigar-shaped mounds, which were built to give the animals somewhere safe and dry to burrow into. The circular enclosure is a much older hillfort, but it too may have been utilised in the rabbit farming process.

Fig. 6.95 Cefn Morfudd, Neath (SS 783973). These square earthworks in the uplands above Neath are something of a mystery. Three can be seen in this view, a fourth is just out of shot, and there is an even larger group further along the ridge to the south. They are all roughly 22m square, and surrounded with a double-bank and ditch. Given that Neath was the site of a major Roman fort the possibility is that these were 'practice camps', but the earthworks lack any characteristic *claviculae* and are too sharply defined to be that old. A plausible suggestion is that they are medieval or post-medieval 'bee gardens' used for honey production. The banks and ditches would have deterred cattle from entering and damaging the straw hives, while the bees spent the summer months feeding off the upland heather blossoms. Similar structures have been recorded in the New Forest (Hampshire).

Fig. 6.96 Neath Abbey (SS 738 973). From this high viewpoint, looking south-east across the site, the ground plan of the abbey is clear. Founded in 1130, the abbey buildings underwent rebuilding during the thirteenth century, and the cruciform church (foreground) would likely have been as magnificent a structure in its day as the broadly contemporary Tintern. The long range bordering the central cloister housed accommodation for the lay brothers (the monks' labour force). On the eve of the Dissolution in 1539 Neath was considered to be the 'fairest abbey in all Wales', but it still came down, although the Abbots House (top right) was reconstructed as a grand mansion in Elizabethan times. This survived until the 1700s when the Industrial Revolution brought copper smelting to the area, and forges were set up within the once-sacred precinct.

Figs **6.97a**, **6.97b** & **6.97c Tintern Abbey** (SO 533 000). The most complete (and arguably the most sublime) of all the monastic sites in Wales is Tintern Abbey, which was founded in 1131 in what was then a sparsely-populated wilderness on the banks of the Wye. With generous backing from the earl of Norfolk and lord of Chepstow, work began in 1270 to transform the modest Norman buildings into the magnificent Gothic structure that stands here today. The cruciform church survived the Reformation remarkably intact, although the extensive claustral buildings on the plain beside the river have fared less well.

This high view from the east overlooks Tintern Abbey and the village, towards the deeply-wooded Angidy valley. The little river flowing through the defile powered the abbey mill at its confluence with the Wye. More surprisingly, this tranquil-looking valley was a hotbed of industrial activity in post-medieval times, the fast-flowing water turning the wheels of a succession of forges, furnaces and workshops. The finished product was then shipped out from a quay beside the abbey.

PREVIOUS SPREAD AND ABOVE: **Figs 6.98a & 6.98b The Cathedral City of St Davids** (SM 751 254). 'And so we came to the end of the world where the patron saint of Wales sleeps by the western sea' wrote Francis Kilvert in his diary in October 1871. This panoramic view eastwards shows the houses – both modern and old – that form the little city on the hill above the medieval close. Legend has it that the church was built down in the hollow to avoid attracting the attention of sea-borne raiders. In the foreground is the hollow shell of the thirteenth- and fourteenth-century Bishop's Palace, dismantled during the Reformation. Just beyond, stands the church that marks the burial place and shrine of the sixth-century saint. The offerings of devout pilgrims who made the long trek to this remote spot, enabled the cathedral to be rebuilt, extended and renovated over many centuries, culminating in the magnificent structure we see here today.

Selected further reading

Aber, J.S., Aber, S.E.W., Marzolff, I. & Ries, J.B., *Small Format Aerial Photography and UAS Imagery* (Elsevier, 2019)

Arnold, J.L. & Davies, J.L., *Roman Wales* (Sutton Publishing, 2000)

Barber, M., *A History of Aerial Photography and Archaeology* (English Heritage, 2011)

Browne, D. & Hughes, S., *Archaeology of the Welsh Uplands* (RCAHMW, 2003)

Davies, J., *A History of Wales* (Penguin, 2007)

Davies, T. & Driver, T., *Historic Wales from the Air* (RCAHMW, 2012)

Davis, P.R., *Forgotten Castles of Wales and the Marches* (Logaston Press, 2023)

Driver, T., *Pembrokeshire, Historic Landscapes from the Air* (RCAHMW, 2007)

—, *The Hillforts of Iron Age Wales* (Logaston Press, 2023)

Fleming, J., *The Welsh Marcher Lordships Vol. 2 (South-West)* (Logaston Press, 2023)

Hilling, J.B., *The Architecture of Wales* (University of Wales Press, 2018)

Hume, P., *The Welsh Marcher Lordships Vol. 1 (Central & North)* (Logaston Press, 2021)

Johnson, A. & K., *Walking the Old Ways of East Breconshire and the Black Mountains* (Logaston Press, 2022)

—, *Walking the Old Ways of Radnorshire* (Logaston Press, 2023)

Lynch, F. & Davies, J.L., *Prehistoric Wales* S. Aldhouse-Green (Sutton Publishing, 2000)

Musson, C., *Montgomeryshire Past and Present from the Air* (The Powysland Club 2011)

—, *Radnorshire from Above, images of landscape and archaeology* (The Radnorshire Society, 2013)

—, *Wales from the Air* (RCAHMW, 1994)

Musson, C. & Driver, T., *Above Brecknock, An historic county from the air* (Brecknock Society / Clwyd-Powys Archaeological Trust / RCAHMW 2015)

Nash, G., *The Architecture of Death, Neolithic chambered tombs in Wales* (Logaston Press, 2006)

Riley, D.N., *Aerial Archaeology in Britain* (Shire Archaeology, 2009)

A panoramic view eastwards over the Iron Age hillfort of Foeldrygarn in the Presel uplands

Index of places

Also from Logaston Press

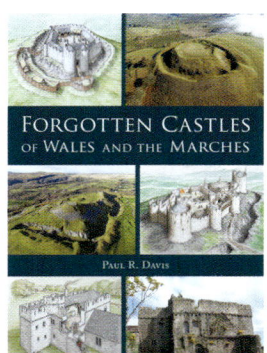

Forgotten Castles of Wales and the Marches PAUL R. DAVIS

'Aimed squarely at the castle enthusiast and visitor ... the visual content is outstanding: stunning aerial views, crisp plans and photographs and ... sharp reconstruction artwork. ... to celebrate the underrated heritage of these sites and the sense of discovery they still evoke.'

– Medieval Archaeology

Wales is a land of castles. The remains of many castles are well cared for by Cadw or English Heritage, but a significant number lie virtually forgotten, solitary on isolated hillsides, buried in sand dunes or hidden in overgrown woodland. Richly illustrated with photographs and reconstructions, this book considers over 60 such castles in detail: why they were built, who was responsible for their construction, the architectural development of their buildings, the causes of their eventual decay and directions to help the reader find what remains can be seen.

152 colour and 59 b&w illus, 8 maps, 3 family trees • 288pp • 242 x 171mm • 2022
ISBN 9781910839522 • PB/ flaps £16.99

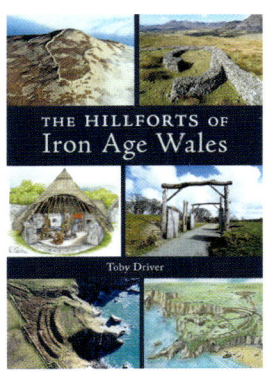

The Hillforts of Iron Age Wales TOBY DRIVER

'Toby Driver is quite the most perfect guide and in *The Hillforts of Iron Age Wales* he combines an easy authority with clear readability, in a book quietly buoyed up by an obvious and communicable enthusiasm for the subject. ... Throughout, it's an absorbing and informing read ... a book that deserves to be on the bookshelf of anyone possessed with more than a passing interest in Wales. It's a quietly marvellous achievement ... a genuine gateway to the past, which Driver has turned into nothing less than an open door.'

– Nation.Cymru

This detailed introduction to the great hillforts, early villages and people of Iron Age Wales showcases the latest research and discoveries alongside the pioneering investigations of early archaeologists. Featuring ground and aerial photographs, vivid reconstructions, maps and plans, the book includes a gazetteer of Iron Age sites to visit and offers detailed tours and access information for ten hillforts of particular interest.

c.200 colour illus, maps & plans • 336pp • 242 x 171mm • 2023 • ISBN 9781910839676 • PB/ flaps £20.00